A Lazy Cook's Summer

mouthwatering recipes
for the time-pressured cook

created by

Lazy Cook Mo Smith

®

A Lazy Cook's Summer

Published in May 2002

by

Lazy Cook Mo Smith
Bear House
Bisley
Stroud
Glos
GL6 7BB

Tel: 01452 770298
Email: info@lazycookmosmith.co.uk
Website: www.lazycookmosmith.co.uk

ISBN 0-9542319-0-2

Written and Edited by
Lazy Cook Mo Smith

Cover Design by Terry Cripps, Easy, Glos.
Printed by Leckhampton Printing Co. Cheltenham, Glos.

to

Helen

William and Lyn

and Edward

Written and Published by the same author

'*A Lazy Cook's Christmas*'
ISBN 1-902100-24-7
price £4.50 per copy (incl. p/p)
(a percentage from each sale is given to charity)

'*Lazy Cook in the Kitchen*'
(recipes from Autumn to Easter)
ISBN 1-902100-23-9
price £6.50 per copy (incl. p/p)
(a percentage from each sale is given to charity)

Copies available from –

Lazy Cook Mo Smith
Bear House
Bisley
Stroud
Glos.
GL6 7BB
tel: 01452 770298
email: info@lazycookmosmith.co.uk
website: www.lazycookmosmith.co.uk

*(cheques made payable to **Lazy Cook Mo Smith**)*

CONTENTS

page

Cookery Abbreviations and Terms (a Lazy Cook's shorthand)   130-131
Complete Index   137-142
Introduction   VI
Lazy Cook's Garden   124-129
Hob and Oven Temperatures   132
Recipes -
    Biscuits/Bread/Cakes/Pastry   1-8
    Canapés   9-11
    Drinks/Cups   12-14
    Fish   15-29
    Icings/Jellies/Syrups   30
    Meat and Poultry   31-47
    Pasta/Rice   48-53
    Preserves – Jam/Chutney/Vinegars   54-61
    Puddings   62-80
    Salads   81-83
    Sauces/Fillings/Pastes – savoury/sweet   84
    Soups/Stocks   85-89
    Starters and Light Meals   90-98
    Vegetables   99-123

Recommended Utensils   133
Recommended Store Cupboard   134-135
Weights and Measures   133

Bear House

A LAZY COOK'S SUMMER

Introduction

Summer to me is all about moving out of the house and into the garden. It is about inviting friends to summer lunches that last well into the afternoon. It is about warm balmy summer evenings drinking Pimm's and everyone cooking supper on a barbecue; it is about summer picnics; it is about relaxing and enjoying the wonder of another new season.

I also recognise that summer can be much more demanding on time and energy than any other season. For one thing it is all too easy to get carried away by the sight of a stall laden with tempting produce forgetting that, unlike winter fruits and vegetables which can be stored for several weeks, most summer ingredients have a short shelf-life and often need to be cooked or eaten the day they are purchased. On the other hand many summer ingredients require little or no cooking at all. My Lazy Cook summer recipes reflect my mood. They keep everything simple, mixing and matching colours and textures; taking a handful of everyday ingredients and transforming them into a meal which is flavoursome and good, and it all happens in so short a time.

Presentation as always is important and most of my recipes can be simply presented for everyday meals, or 'dressed up' for a special celebration. Planning is important too even if it involves little more than making a shopping list and I hope you will find my Recommended Store-cupboard a help. The right tool for the right job is as important for cooking as for any craft and the items under Recommended Kitchen Equipment might help you to avoid cluttering up your cupboards.

If you are becoming increasingly concerned about the ingredients you buy, how they are grown; from where they come, you might like to venture into a little gardening even if it extends no further than your kitchen windowsill or balcony patio. My chapter headed 'A Lazy Cook's Garden' might give the encouragement you need to have a go.

Above all, relax, delight your family and friends this summer with Lazy Cook recipes. All too soon the flowers will lose their splendour and the leaves will begin to fall. Time to put the garden to bed, to move back indoors and look forward to the temptations the autumn has on offer – jacket potatoes, hot soups and Sunday roasts – enjoy them all.

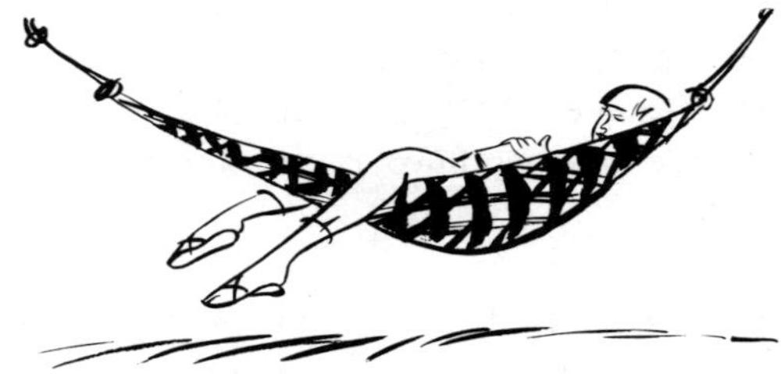

BISCUITS/BREAD/CAKES

BISCUITS

Almond Biscuits

to make approx. 30
175gms (6 ozs) butter – softened
100gms (4ozs) caster sugar
100gms (4ozs) plain flour
50gms (2ozs) ground almonds
few spots almond essence

Set oven at gas 4/400°f/200°c/Aga baking oven.   Lightly oil a baking tray. Put the flour and sugar into a food processor and process for a few seconds.   Add the ground almonds, butter and essence and process for a few seconds to blend together. Put teaspoons of the mixture on to the prepared tray, spaced a little apart, and flatten each with a wet fork.   Bake in the pre-set oven for 15-20mins. or until they become biscuit in colour. Cool on a wire tray, store in an airtight tin.

Chocolate and Cinnamon Biscuits

to make approx. 40
175gms. (6ozs) margarine – softened
175gms (6ozs) plain flour
25gms (1oz) drinking chocolate
25gms (1oz) semolina
75gms (3ozs) soft brown sugar
1 teas. ground cinnamon

Set oven at gas 4/400°f/200°c/Aga baking oven
Lightly oil a baking tray.   Put the flour, drinking chocolate, semolina, sugar and cinnamon powder into a food processor and process for a few seconds.   Add the softened margarine and process for a few seconds to blend together.   Put teaspoonsful of the mixture on to the prepared tray, spaced a little apart, and flatten each with a wet fork.   Bake in the pre-set oven for 20-30mins. or until they become crisp.   Cool on a wire tray, store in an airtight tin.

Lemon Biscuits

to make approx. 40
175gms (6ozs) margarine – softened
250gms (8ozs) plain white flour
75gms (3ozs) granulated sugar
grated rind of one lemon
3tbls. fresh lemon juice

Set oven at gas 4/400°f/200°c/Aga baking oven.   Lightly oil a baking tray.
Put the flour and sugar into a food processor and process for a few
seconds.   Add the remaining ingredients and process for a few seconds to
blend together. Put teaspoonsful of the mixture on to the prepared tray,
spaced a little apart, and flatten each with a fork dipped in fresh lemon
juice.   Bake in the pre-set oven for 20-30mins. or until they begin to turn a
biscuit colour.   Cool on a wire tray, store in an airtight tin.

Spicy Fruit Biscuits

to make approx. 40
175gms (6ozs) margarine – softened
250gms (8ozs) plain white flour
75gms (3ozs) demerara sugar
1 teas. mixed spice
125gms (4ozs) raisins
2 tbls. milk

Set oven at gas 4/400°f/200°c/Aga baking oven.
Lightly oil a baking tray.   Put the flour, sugar and spice into a food
processor and process for a few seconds before adding the softened
margarine, raisins and milk and process for a few seconds to blend
together.   Put teaspoonsful of the mixture on to the prepared tray, spaced a
little apart, and flatten each with a wet fork.   Bake in the pre-set oven for
20-30mins. or until they begin to turn a biscuit colour.   Cool on a wire
tray, store in an airtight tin.

BREADS AND ROLLS

Evy's Fruit Loaf

300gms (10ozs) plain flour
2 teas. baking powder
75gms. (3 ozs) caster sugar
1 large egg
100gms (4ozs) mixed dried fruit
225ml (8ozs) full cream milk

Set oven at gas 4/400°f/200°c/Aga baking oven.   Line the base and ends of a 900gm. (2 lb) loaf tin with a strip of greaseproof and oil all over.   Put the flour, baking powder and sugar into a food processor and process for a few seconds.   Add the egg, mixed fruit and milk and process until smooth. Pour into the prepared tin and bake in the pre-set oven for 30-40mins. or until set (test with a skewer - if it comes out clean the loaf is baked). Remove from tin and cool on a wire tray.   To serve, slice thickly and spread with butter.

Lazy Cook tips – *do not process for too long once the fruit has been added. This recipe was given to me by Evy, a relative and a superb cook.   It is best made and eaten the same day.   If stored, put into a polythene bag in a refrigerator and serve within 2 days, or freeze.*

Bread and Rolls - *although bread making is not usually associated with lazy cooking, prepared the **Lazy Cook** way it is a really quick process.*

White Rolls and Bread

to make 12-16 rolls or 1 x 500gm (1 lb) loaf

25gms (1 oz) fresh yeast
1 teas. sugar
warm water
500gms (1 lb) strong white flour
50gms (2ozs) butter, margarine or lard – cut up

Set oven at gas 6/450°f/220°c/Aga roasting oven.   Lightly oil a baking tray.
Put the yeast and sugar into a measuring jug, add a little warm water and mix it to a smooth paste before adding more warm water to bring it up to 300ml. (½pt); and stir. ✳ Put the flour and fat into a food processor and process for a few seconds to work in the fat then pour on the yeast liquid and stop the processor when it forms a dough.   Put on to a lightly floured board and knead together until smooth (about a minute).

To make rolls - cut the dough into 12 or 16 pieces, place on baking tray and leave until they double in size.   Put into the pre-set oven and bake for 10mins. before reducing the oven temperature to gas 4/400°f/200°c/Aga – place on a lower shelf.   Continue to bake for a further 5-10mins. (when done they should sound hollow when tapped on the base).   Cool on a wire tray.   Serve warm or cold.   Store in a polythene bag in the refrigerator or freeze until required.

To make a loaf - shape the kneaded dough into a round and put on a baking tray.   When double in size bake as for rolls.

Lazy Cook tips – *1-2tbls. oil can be added in place of the fat listed.   Other flavouring ingredients can also be added i.e. olives, sundried tomatoes etc. I prefer to use fresh yeast, available from Bakers, Delicatessen, and Health Food Shops, it can be frozen.   I do not recommend more than a 500gm (1 lb) quantity is mixed in a food processor at any one time.   With practice the whole process can take as little as 10mins preparation time.*

Wholemeal Rolls and Bread

to make 12-16 rolls
25gms (1 oz) fresh yeast
1 teas. sugar
1 desst. molasses
warm water
225gms (8ozs) strong white flour
225gms (8ozs) wholemeal flour
50gms (2ozs) butter, margarine or lard – cut up

Set oven at gas 6/450°f/220°c/Aga roasting oven. Lightly oil a baking tray. Put the yeast and sugar into a measuring jug, add a little warm water and mix it to a smooth paste before adding the molasses and more warm water to bring it to just over 300ml. (½pt) quantity and stir. Follow the directions for white rolls and a loaf from ✱ on page 4.

Lazy Cook tips - wholemeal flour absorbs more liquid than white flour and you will need to increase the amount of water added to the yeast mixture possibly by as much as 25mls. (1 fl. oz). Wholemeal dough should be of a 'slippery' consistency, the exact amount of water required will be found with practice.

Breadcrumbs - fresh or dried

Put pieces of bread (brown or white) into a food processor or liquidiser and process until crumbed. Use immediately or dry them on a tin tray in a cool oven or on top of an Aga. Store in airtight jars, they will keep for months.

Lazy Cook tips - a most useful ingredient to have in store. Use for coating ingredients before cooking; for topping savoury and sweet dishes, or for thickening soups.

CAKES

Chocolate Cake

100gms (4ozs) plain flour
1 teas. baking powder
75gms (3ozs) demerara or soft brown sugar
50gms (2ozs) drinking chocolate
2 large eggs
125gms (5ozs) butter – softened
50gms (2ozs) ground almonds

Set oven at gas 4/400°f/200°c/Aga baking oven. Line the base of a 17/20cm (7"/8") round cake tin and lightly oil all over. Put the flour, baking powder, sugar and drinking chocolate into a food processor and process for a few seconds. Add all remaining ingredients and process until smooth. Pour into the prepared tin and bake for 30-40mins. or until set. Allow to cool a little before turning on to a wire tray (top uppermost). Slice to serve when cold. Store in an airtight tin or freeze.

Lazy Cook tips – this is a moist, rich cake. It can be made into a dessert – see 'Chocolate and Strawberry Gateau' recipe on page 62.

Coffee and Cinnamon Cake

175gms (6ozs) margarine – softened
225gms (8ozs) plain flour
2 teas. baking powder
175gms (6ozs) soft brown sugar
1 teas. ground cinnamon
3 large eggs
1 desst. Camp Coffee Essence
1 tbls. hot water
topping
1 teas. freshly ground coffee
½ teas. ground cinnamon
2 teas. demerara sugar

Set oven at gas 4/400°f/200°c/Aga baking oven.

Line the base and ends of a 900gm (2 lb) loaf tin with greaseproof and oil all over lightly. Put the flour, baking powder, sugar and ground cinnamon into a food processor and process for a few seconds. Add remaining ingredients (not the topping), and process for a few seconds until smooth. Pour into the prepared tin and smooth the top. Mix the topping ingredients together and scatter over the cake mixture before baking in the pre-set oven for 40-45mins. or until set (test with a skewer - if it comes out clean the cake is baked). Cool a little before removing from the tin and cooling on a wire tray. Slice to serve. Store in an airtight tin or polythene bag, or freeze until required – defrost before serving.

Lazy Cook tips – if you do not have freshly ground coffee for the topping use coffee granules. To remove the cake from the tin, loosen the sides with a palette knife and pull the greaseproof ends and lift. A cake with unusual but good flavours

Lemon Cake

250gms (8ozs) butter – softened
250gms (8ozs) plain white flour
2 teas. baking powder
175gms. (6ozs) caster sugar
3 large eggs
100ml. (4 fl.ozs) single cream
grated zest of 2 lemons
4tbls. lemon juice

Set oven at gas 4/400°f/200°c/Aga baking oven.

Line the base and ends of a 900gm (2 lb) loaf tin with greaseproof and oil lightly. Put the flour, baking powder and sugar into a food processor and process for a few seconds before adding the softened butter, eggs, single cream, lemon zest and 1 tbls. lemon juice and process for a few seconds until smooth. Pour into the prepared tin, smooth the top and bake in the pre-set oven for 40-45mins. or until set. Cool a little before removing from the tin on to a wire tray and before it is completely cold prick the top with a metal skewer and pour 2-3tbls. fresh lemon juice into the cake. Slice to serve when the cake is cold. Store in an airtight tin or polythene bag.

Lazy Cook tips – *a light moist cake with a good lemon flavour. To remove the cake from the tin, loosen the sides with a palette knife and pull the greaseproof ends and lift.*

Lemon Sandwich/Gateau

100gms (4ozs) plain flour
1 teas. baking powder
75gms (3 ozs) caster sugar
100gms (4ozs) butter or margarine - soften
3 eggs
filling –
½ jar lemon curd
fresh lemon juice

Set oven at gas 4/400°f/200°c/Aga baking oven. Lightly grease or oil 2 x 17cm (7") sandwich tins. Put the flour, baking powder and sugar into a food processor and process for a few seconds, add the fat and eggs and process for a few seconds until smooth. Spread between the sandwich tins and bake in the pre-set oven for 20-30mins. or until set. Remove from oven and leave for a minute or two before turning on to a wire tray, pour lemon juice into each cake then leave to cool. Mix lemon juice into the lemon curd and sandwich the cakes together with this. Scatter the top with caster sugar and slice to serve.

Lazy Cook tips – *I use sandwich tins which belonged to my Mother in Law – they have a metal strip secured in the centre and by turning this round the tin the sandwich is easily removed when baked. Make this into a luxury cake by sandwiching the cakes with lemon curd and whipped cream and spreading the top with lemon icing (recipe below).*

Lemon Icing

100gms (4 ozs) icing sugar
lemon juice
lemon zest

Sieve the icing sugar into a bowl and mix to a paste with lemon juice. Spread on to the cake and scatter with lemon zest.

CANAPES

Melon and Fruit Sticks

Cut a melon in half, discard the seeds, scoop out the flesh with a teaspoon. Spike the melon pieces on to cocktail sticks with other fruits i.e.
peach slice
whole strawberry
cherry
raspberry
grape
slice of nectarine

Spike on to the upturned melon case and hand round to serve.

Lazy Cook tips – these are most refreshing canapés to serve. With additional ingredients they can be served as starters, see recipe, page 93.

Pastry Bases

to make 40-50
100gms (4ozs) plain white flour
100gms (4ozs) wholemeal flour
100gms (4ozs) lard
2-3fl.oz cold water

Set oven at gas 6/450°f/220°c/Aga roasting oven.
Put the flours into a food processor and process for a few seconds. Add the lard in pieces, switch on processor and after a few seconds pour the liquid through the funnel until a ball of pastry is formed, switch off. Roll the pastry on a lightly floured board to approximately 4mm (¼") thickness and cut into rounds using a 3½cm (1½") diameter plain cutter. Place on baking trays, prick lightly with a fork and bake for 10-15mins. or until they begin to change colour. Cool on a wire tray and store in an airtight container. Use within 1 month, or freeze.

Lazy Cook tips – these little bases are a wonderful asset to have in store. They can be served, topped with numerous ingredients as canapés, or two or three can be served as a starter. Make from shortcrust or wholemeal pastry; home-made or ready made from a supermarket.

Pastry Bases topped with Herb Cheese and Fresh Strawberries

pastry bases (recipe page 9)
cream cheese
fresh parsley – chopped
fresh strawberries
chives

Soften the cheese and work in the chopped parsley.   Pile on to the pastry bases, top with a strawberry and 'spike' with strips of chive.

Lazy Cook tips – make with full-fat, reduced-fat cheeses or Quark.   A few spots of milk will help the cheese 'softening' process.   Serve three of these with a little mixed green salad as a starter.

Pastry Bases topped with Savoury Butter, Black Pudding and Tomato

pastry bases (recipe page 9)
butter - softened
tomato purée
black pudding – remove skin
tomatoes - slice
fresh mixed herbs - chop

Work a little tomato purée into the softened butter and spread it over each pastry base.   Top with a slice of black pudding then a slice of tomato and sprinkle with fresh chopped herbs.

Lazy Cook tips – serve as canapés or serve 3 as a starter with a little mixed salad.

Pastry Bases topped with Savoury Butter, Ox Tongue and Cornichons

pastry bases (recipe page 9)
butter - softened
whole grain mustard
ox tongue slices
cornichons
black pepper

Work a little made mustard into the softened butter and spread it over each pastry base. Cut the ox tongue into strips and wrap around a whole cornichon before placing on the buttered pastry base. Season with a little freshly ground pepper.

Lazy Cook tips – *cornichons (or cocktail gherkins) can be bought in supermarkets or delicatessen and are a useful ingredient to have in store. Serve three of these canapés as a starter with a little mixed green salad.*

<u>Chicken Liver Parcels</u> - *recipe page 90.*

<u>Cherry Tomatoes with a Savoury Filling</u> - *recipe page 118.*

<u>Fresh Salmon Bake</u> - *recipe page 26.*

DRINKS/WINE CUPS

Elderflower Cordial

makes approx. 2ltrs (5pts)
20 large ripe elderflower heads
2 fresh lemons – sliced
900gms (2 lbs) granulated sugar
1½ ozs citric acid crystals
2¼ltrs (4pts) boiling water

Wash the elderflower heads and put with remaining ingredients into a large bowl and stir until the sugar has dissolved. Cover and leave overnight. Strain and pour into bottles and store in a refrigerator. Dilute with water to serve.

Lazy Cook tips – elderflower cordials have become very popular and can be purchased from most supermarkets and delicatessen. Even so, if fresh elderflowers are accessible to you the above recipe is quick and trouble free and makes a good quantity of very refreshing cordial. Poured into ice cubes it can be frozen. The elderflower season is a short one, watch the trees daily because the flowers soon loose their ripeness. I was given this recipe by a village friend.

Herb Flavoured Water - to make daily

Wash a collection of fresh herbs to include, marjoram or oregano, lemon balm, mint and parsley
fresh lemon slices
water

Stir all together in a jug and store in a refrigerator. Strain to serve throughout the day.

Lazy Cook tips – this is best made with herbs picked on the stalk, fresh from the garden, it is most refreshing.

Iced Coffee

Make a jug of extra strong coffee using grounds or granules and when cold put it into a refrigerator to chill. Serve straight from the refrigerator topped with full cream milk or cream – single or whipped.

Lazy Cook tips – the coffee must be made extra strong, I make it with freshly ground beans topped up with boiling water and stirred well. Iced Coffee is refreshing and delicious served on a hot day.

Lemonade

to make approx 2pts
4 lemons
3 tbls. granulated sugar
1 ltr. (1¾pts) boiling water
sprigs of mint
ice

Wash and scrub 3 of the lemons before cutting into pieces. Put into a large bowl, add the sugar and pour on the boiling water, stir and leave for 20-30mins. Strain into a jug and when cold store, covered, in a refrigerator. Just before serving stir in several small sprigs of fresh mint, several slices of lemon and ice.

Lazy Cook tips – a most refreshing drink to serve in summer. Use within 5 days.

WINE CUPS

Pimm's

serves approx. 20 x 300ml./½pt tumblers
1 ltr. bottle Pimm's No. 1
300ml (½ pt) dry ginger ale
2 ltrs. lemonade
cucumber slices
orange slices
strawberries
sprigs of mint
lemon balm
ice

Mix all together and serve.

Sparkling Cup

serves approx. 12 wine glasses
1 bottle sparkling wine
50ml. (2ozs) Grand Marnier
50ml. (2ozs) brandy
600ml. (1pt) lemonade
peach and nectarine slices
ice

Mix all the ingredients together and serve.

Summer sunshine

serves approx. 24 wine glasses
3 bottles dry white wine
¼ bottle of cognac or brandy
9 tbls. Benedictine (or orange Curaçao or Crème de Menthe)
1 tin (454gms) pineapple pieces
1 ltr. (1¾ pts) fizzy lemonade
ice
Mix all together and serve.

FISH

Cod Fillet baked with Almonds and served with a Fresh Plum Sauce

to serve 4
700gms (1½ lbs) fillet of cod
25gms (1oz) butter
fresh plum sauce (recipe below)
50gms (2ozs) flaked almonds – lightly browned

Set oven at gas 6/450°/220°c/Aga roasting oven.
Cover the base of a shallow ovenproof dish with a film of cold water. Wash and dry the fish, put into the dish, skin side down, and top with shavings of butter then with flaked almonds. Bake in the pre-set oven for 10-15mins. or until the fish is firm to the touch. Serve straight from the baking dish or put the fish down the centre of a hot serving dish and pour some of the plum sauce around, serve the remainder separately. While the fish is baking make the sauce.

Lazy Cook tips – the fish can be baked in one piece or cut into portions – a whole fillet will take longer to bake than smaller pieces. The sauce can be made while the fish is baking, it should not be sweet, just slightly tart in flavour. The combined flavours are excellent. Always keep a supply of lightly browned flaked almonds in stock – brown in the oven or under a grill and store in a jar or airtight container.

Fresh Plum Sauce

900gms (2lbs) plums – stone and slice
50ml (2ozs) Sweet Martini
runny honey to taste
a few drops almond essence

Simmer the plum slices in a pan with the Martini until they begin to soften, lid on pan. Taste, stir in a little runny honey if the flavour is too sharp, then stir in 2-3 drops almond essence. Serve hot or cold with fish, meat or poultry.

Lazy Cook tips – make with Victoria plums when available. It should be slightly sharp in flavour.

Concertinas of Fish

makes 4
4 fillets of white fish (plaice or sole)
3-4 fresh tomatoes
fresh basil leaves
cocktail sticks
a little oil
freshly ground white pepper
a little white wine – optional

Set oven at gas 6/450°f/220°c/Aga roasting oven.
Cover the base of a shallow ovenproof dish with a film of white wine (or water).   Gather each fillet into a concertina shape and between each fold tuck a slice of tomato and a basil leaf.   Secure into shape with a cocktail stick and pack into the prepared dish.   Brush lightly with oil and season with a little freshly ground white pepper.   Bake in the pre-set oven for 10-15mins. or until firm to the touch.   To serve, put the concertinas on to a hot serving dish and remove the cocktail sticks.

Lazy Cook tips – to avoid the tomato slices protruding too high above the fish it may be necessary to cut the slices in half.   This is a most colourful way to present fish and the flavours are delicate and delicious.   They can be barbecued by placing the prepared concertinas on to lightly oiled foil.

Fish Pudding

to serve 4
300ml (½pt) milk
1 medium onion – skin and chop
several good pinches ground clove
freshly ground white pepper
500gms (1 lb) skinless white fish fillet (or smoked haddock)
2 large eggs
175gms (6ozs) grated cheese
fresh parsley – chopped
6-8 slices bread and butter (medium sliced)

Warm a little of the milk in a pan over a gentle heat, add the ground clove, the pepper and the prepared onion, place the fish on top and simmer, with lid on pan, for approximately 5mins. Break up the fish. Butter, or oil a 1lt. (or 2pt) soufflé, or pie dish, and line the base with bread and butter, top with a layer of the fish and onion mixture (removing it with a slotted spoon), some of the parsley and cheese, then top with bread and butter and continue layering until all the ingredients are used ending with bread and butter topped with cheese and parsley. Add the remaining milk to the pan juices and warm. Whisk the eggs, pour on the milk and whisk again before pouring through a sieve on to the pudding. Press the ingredients down with a fork and, if possible, leave for 30mins. to 1 hour before baking in a pre-set oven (gas 4/400°f/200°c/Aga baking oven for 30-40mins.) or until well risen and brown on top. Serve hot.

Lazy Cook tips – *make this in a basin if you do not have a soufflé or pie dish. Use up odd ends of cheese, mix the flavours but grate soft cheeses before hard ones. This recipe can also be made with shell fish.*

Baked Gurnard with a Savoury Paste Filling

to serve 2
1 whole gurnard - gutted
a little white wine
a little olive oil
savoury paste (recipe page 18)

Wipe the fish with kitchen roll before filling with savoury paste. Sew with strong thread or secure with cocktail sticks and place in a shallow ovenproof dish the base of which has been moistened with a film of white wine (or water). Brush the skin with olive oil before baking in the pre-set oven for approx. 30mins. or until the fish is firm to the touch. Serve hot or cold.

Lazy Cook tips – *don't let the appearance of gurnard put you off buying it - it has pure white, almost flaky flesh, and lots of flavour. It is inexpensive compared with most white fish – request it from your fishmonger or supermarket counter.*

Savoury Paste – *for fish, meat, poultry or vegetables*

50gms (2ozs) bread – brown or white
25gms (1oz) cooked ham
8 anchovy fillets
6 black olives – pitted
2 sundried tomatoes – preserved in oil
2 teas. pesto
1 desst. oil – from the jar of sundried tomatoes
freshly ground white pepper

Put the bread and ham into a food processor (or liquidiser), and process until a breadcrumb texture.   Add all remaining ingredients and process until they form a sticky paste.   Use immediately or store, in a covered container in a refrigerator, use within 3 days.

Lazy Cook tips – I recommend anchovy fillets preserved in oil and bought by weight from most supermarkets or delicatessen counters.

Herring Fillets baked in Orange Juice

to serve 4
4 herring fillets
8-12 anchovies preserved in oil
fresh coriander
50ml (2fl.ozs) white wine
50ml (2fl.ozs) fresh orange juice (from a carton)
1 teas. tomato purée

Set oven at gas 6/450°f/220°c/Aga roasting oven.
Wipe the fillets with kitchen roll, cut off and discard the fins, and place the fillets, skin side down, in a shallow ovenproof dish and top each fillet with 2 or 3 anchovies.   Put the wine and orange juice into a small pan and whisk in the tomato purée, bring to boiling point then pour over the herring fillets and scatter with fresh coriander.   Bake, uncovered, for 7-10mins. or until the fillets are firm to the touch.   Serve hot or cold, with seasonal vegetables or salad.

Lazy Cook tips – *herring fillets are cheap and nutritious.   This is just one of many ways I serve them.   I recommend anchovy fillets preserved in oil and bought by weight from most supermarkets or delicatessen counters.   A small tin of Britvic orange juice is a perfect size for this recipe, a useful store-cupboard ingredient – quick to use and no waste.*

Mackerel Fillets baked in White Wine – to serve cold

to serve 4
4 mackerel fillets
150ml (¼pt) white wine
150ml (¼pt) fish stock
1 lemon
2 onion slices
a few strands of fresh fennel fern
6 white peppercorns
1 dried bayleaf
1 teas. Dijon mustard
fresh parsley

Set oven at gas 6/450°f/220°c/Aga baking oven.
Wipe the mackerel fillets with kitchen roll and cut off and discard the fins. Put the fillets into a shallow ovenproof dish, skin side down.   Put the wine, stock, a slice of lemon peel, 1 tbls. lemon juice, the onion slices, fennel fern, peppercorns and bayleaf into a pan and boil for a minute or two, without lid to reduce a little.   Strain on to the fillets and bake in the pre-set oven for 5-10mins. or until the fillets are firm to the touch.   Place the fillets down the centre of a serving dish, whisk the mustard into the cooking liquid and pour it over the fillets.   Leave to become cold and scatter with freshly chopped parsley to serve.

Lazy Cook tips – *if a bought fish stock is used, I suggest 2/3rds wine and 1/3rd stock.   For home-made stock see page 89.   This is a favourite summer fish recipe.   Serve it with fresh bread or rolls, or with salad and new potatoes for a more substantial summer lunch.   This recipe is best made the day before it is needed, store it, covered, in a refrigerator until required.   Bring back to room temperature to serve.   Eat within 4 days*

Mediterranean Fish Pie

to serve 4-6
4 slices of medium sliced bread – break into pieces
100gms (4ozs) pancetta (bacon) – cut up
8-10 anchovy fillets preserved in oil
50gms (2ozs) black pitted olives
6 sundried tomatoes
1 x 227g. tin chopped tomatoes
1 teas. sundried tomato purée
50ml. (2ozs) water
1 teas. fresh rosemary
1-2 cloves garlic – chopped or crushed
freshly ground black pepper
4 mackerel fillets (or any fish fillets of your choice)
garnish –
freshly chopped parsley

Set oven at gas 6/450°f/220°c/Aga roasting oven.
With the exception of the fish and the garnish, put all the remaining ingredients into a food processor or liquidiser and process for a few seconds to make into a rough paste. Lightly oil the base of a shallow ovenproof dish and spread the paste over the base, put the fish fillets on top and bake, uncovered, in the pre-set oven for 10-15mins. or until the fish is firm to the touch. Scatter with chopped parsley to serve.

Lazy Cook tips *– if white fish fillets are used, brush with a little oil from the jar of sundried tomatoes before baking. I recommend anchovy fillets preserved in oil and available from delicatessen and supermarkets by weight.*

Prawn and Melon Platter

This recipe can be served as a simple starter or 'dressed up' for a special occasion.

to serve 6 as a starter
1 large honeydew melon
500gms (1 lb) fresh cooked prawns (without shells)
 lettuce leaves
12 whole prawns complete with shells and heads
parsley sprigs

Cut the melon in half lengthways, remove and discard the seeds. Using a melon baller, or a teaspoon, remove the melon flesh, mix it with the peeled prawns and pile it back into the melon cases with any juices which may have escaped, garnish with parsley sprigs. 'Hang' 6 whole prawns round the edge of each melon. To serve, stand each melon half on lettuce leaves on separate serving plates, pass them round the table for guests to help themselves. Serve with brown bread and butter and mayonnaise.

Lazy Cook tips - I suggest honeydew melon but, with the exception of water melon, any large melon can be used for this recipe. There should be enough filling for it to rise above the melon cases.

For a more eye-catching presentation for serving this recipe as part of a buffet table for a special lunch or celebration party, garnish them as follows –
Cover the base of two large serving dishes (or trays covered with foil), with shredded lettuce and place a filled melon in the centre of each. Stand 8-10 avocado slices against the side of the melon cases and put a half hard-boiled egg at the end of each (to resemble oars of a boat).   Put a shelled prawn on each egg and scatter lightly with paprika.   Tie 4 or 5 whole prawns in shells into a bunch, (tie them with a chive) and place one on top of each melon.

Lazy Cook tips – to prevent avocado slices discolouring, always cut them using a stainless steel knife. Remember to cut them in half and remove the centre stone before peeling.

Fresh Salmon

Fresh salmon is for me one of the nicest if all summer ingredients. Although it is no longer the luxury it once was a whole fresh salmon presented in the way I recommend will take pride of place on a summer buffet table. There are so many ways of serving fresh salmon but the important thing to remember is not to overcook it, this will spoil the delicate flavour, my motto is – 'undercooked fish is unpalatable, but overcooked salmon is a disaster'. Whether the salmon is baked whole or in pieces, it should be moist and creamy but so often it is dry and flavourless. The following recipes illustrate just a few ways I serve fresh salmon in summer.

To bake a whole Salmon

For a whole salmon, minimum weight including head and tail, 1¾kg (4 lbs), allow 10mins. per 500gms (1 lb), i.e. a salmon weighing 1¾kg (4 lbs) needs 40mins. baking.

Set the oven at gas mark 6/450°f/220°c/Aga roasting oven.
Wrap the salmon in a piece of well buttered greaseproof then wrap it in foil. Place it in a meat tin (or ovenproof dish), and pour in boiling water to come half way up the parcel. Put it in the pre-set oven and half way through the baking time turn the parcel over so that the upper half is now in the water for the remainder of the baking time. Remove from oven, drain off the liquid and leave the salmon in the parcel until it is cold. Serve, or store in a fridge or cold larder, (in the cooking parcel). Serve within 4 days.

Baked Salmon with a Savoury Jelly garnish – to serve cold

1¾kg (4 lb) salmon should serve 10-12 portions
2½kg (6 lb) salmon should serve 20-25 portions
1 whole baked salmon - cold (recipe above)
½ a cucumber
3 lemons
parsley sprig
savoury jelly (recipe page 23)

Peel off the skin and place the salmon, including head and tail, down the centre of a large serving dish (or a tray covered with foil). Place slices of cucumber down the centre of the salmon, and lemon slices, cut in half, around the salmon (cut side nearest the salmon). Surround with chopped savoury jelly and place a parsley sprig in the eye socket. Serve with mayonnaise (recipe page 26), new potatoes, mixed green salad, Tomato Salad (recipe page 83) and fresh rolls for a delicious summer lunch.

Lazy Cook tips - if the whole salmon is to be served hot allow an extra 10mins. to the overall baking time and test by opening the parcel, remove the fin from the thickest part of the salmon at the centre back and examine the flesh which should be firm but moist.

Savoury Jelly

to make 600ml (1 pt)
300ml (½pt) dry white wine
1 bayleaf
12 black peppercorns
4 whole cloves
a few strips of lemon rind
1 tbls. white wine vinegar
1 sachet gelatine

Put the wine, bayleaf, peppercorns, cloves and lemon rind into a pan and boil for a minute, remove from heat and add 1 tbls. white wine vinegar. Sprinkle the gelatine on to 300ml (½pt) hot water and whisk until it has dissolved. Strain the wine through a fine sieve on to the gelatine mixture, stir well and when cold cover and put into a refrigerator or cold larder to set. Use within 4 days. To chop, turn the set jelly on to a piece of wet greaseproof paper and chop it with a sharp wet knife – as it chops it sparkles like diamonds.

Lazy Cook tips – change the flavour by adding one of the many herb flavoured vinegars now on sale, change the colour by using red wine. Leaf gelatine can be used, follow the manufacturer's instructions to use. Chopped jelly will add instant splendour to all savoury dishes.

Fresh Salmon Millefeuille

to serve 6-8
250gms. (8ozs) ready rolled puff pastry
500gms. (1 lb) cooked salmon (recipe page 22)
mayonnaise (recipe page 26)
fresh lemon juice
1-2tbls. freshly chopped parsley
garnish -
cucumber slices
lemon slices

Set oven at gas 7/475°f/230°c/Aga roasting oven.
Cut the pastry into two pieces, place on a wet baking tray, prick all over with a fork and bake in the pre-set oven for 8-10mins. or until the pastry has risen and is brown on top.   Turn the pastry over and bake for a further 5-10mins or until cooked.   Remove from oven and cool on a wire tray. To assemble, put one piece of cooked pastry on to a serving dish (or a tray covered with foil).   Break the salmon into mouth-sized pieces and stir into several tablespoons of mayonnaise, with a good sprinkling of lemon juice and chopped parsley.   Spread between the two pieces of pastry and garnish the top with cucumber and lemon slices.   Slice to serve.

Lazy Cook tips – ready-made and rolled puff pastry can be purchased from supermarkets. Always keep some in a freezer and follow the directions on the packet for thawing and baking. Home-made mayonnaise is best but in a real emergency use a good quality bought one. For a more eye-catching presentation arrange strips of smoked salmon on the top in a lattice pattern and fill the centres with lemon pieces, fresh strawberries (wild ones if available), and parsley sprigs.

Fresh Salmon Roulade

to serve 8-10 slices
1 cooked roulade – recipe
filling -
500gms (1 lb) fresh salmon – cooked (recipe page 22)
2 tbls. freshly chopped parsley
300ml (½pt) mayonnaise (recipe page 26)
cucumber slices

Spread the roulade with mayonnaise, top with salmon (flaked into pieces) and scatter with chopped parsley. Lift the teacloth and greaseproof and roll the roulade on to a large serving dish. Garnish by placing cucumber slices down the centre, slice to serve.

Lazy Cook tips - is one of the most delicious summer meals I serve, the texture is light and the flavours excellent. Serve it with a green salad, a tomato salad and fresh bread or rolls. Refer to 'Lazy Cook tips' under the 'Roulade' recipe below for other filling suggestions.

Roulade

to serve 8-10 slices
100gms (4ozs) butter
100gms (4ozs) plain flour
4 large eggs – separated
600ml (1pt) full cream milk
several pinches cayenne pepper

Set oven at gas 4/400°f/200°c/Aga baking oven.
Line a swiss roll tin with well buttered greaseproof paper to protrude above the tin by 5cms. (2"). Melt the butter in a large saucepan, add the flour and mix into a paste before adding the milk, stir continuously until the mixture simmers and thickens (like a thick sauce). Allow to cool a little before pouring adding the egg yolks and the cayenne and mixing to a smooth paste (this can be done in a food processor). Whisk the egg whites in a large bowl or basin until they are stiff, and fold in the sauce. Pour into the prepared tin, smooth the top and bake in the pre-set oven for 30-40mins. or until it has risen and is golden on top. Remove from oven and turn on to a piece of greaseproof paper with a folded teacloth beneath, remove the greaseproof in which it was baked and leave until cold – use a palette knife to ease the paper from the roulade.

Lazy Cook tips – when lining the tin it is important that the paper protrudes above the tin to accommodate the roulade which rises as it bakes. In addition to the salmon filling this roulade can be prepared with other savoury and sweet fillings. Cooked spinach, or a variety of cooked mushrooms make excellent vegetarian meals. Cream and berries provide a delicious pudding

Fresh Salmon Bake

1 cooked roulade (recipe page 25)
filling -
500gms (1 lb) fresh salmon – cooked (recipe page 22)
300ml (½pt) mayonnaise (recipe page 26)
2 tbls. freshly chopped parsley

Spread the roulade with mayonnaise, top with salmon (flaked into pieces) and scatter with chopped parsley.   Cut into wedges and serve.

Lazy Cook tips – *cut into wedges of various sizes to serve as canapés, starters or main courses.*

Mayonnaise

to make approx. 300ml (½pt)
1 large egg
2 desst. wine vinegar
¼ teas. of each of the following – salt, ground white pepper, mustard powder
oil – approx. 300ml (½pt)

Break the egg into a food processor or liquidiser and add the vinegar, salt, pepper and mustard powder.   Process together for a few seconds before gradually pouring in the oil until until it thickens – the more oil you add the thicker it will become.   Store in a covered jar and keep in the refrigerator.   Use within 7 days.

Lazy Cook tips - *there is no substitute for home made mayonnaise and with the aid of a food processor or liquidiser it is made in minutes..   I use sunflower oil but others can be used.   Different flavoured vinegars can also be used.   It is a most useful ingredient to have in store.*

Smoked Salmon and Prawn Parcels with a Creamed Pepper Sauce

to make 4
4 slices smoked salmon
3 tbls. double cream
2 teas. grain mustard
a few pinches ground white pepper
1 teas. horseradish cream
100gms (4ozs) cooked prawns
1 hard boiled egg - chopped
freshly chopped parsley
chives
1 pkt. peppered Boursin cheese
1-2 tbls. milk

Add the mustard, pepper and horseradish to the cream and whip to a soft peak. Stir in the prawns, chopped egg and parsley and pile into the centre of each smoked salmon slice then gather together (like a pouch) and secure by tying with a strand of chive. Put the Boursin and milk into a pan and stir together over a gentle heat until the Boursin has melted and the consistency is runny. To serve, place the salmon pouches down the centre of a serving dish (or on individual plates) and pour the Boursin round.

Lazy Cook tips –*serve this recipe as a starter with fresh bread or brown bread and butter, or serve as a light lunch with salad and fresh bread or rolls. Melted Boursin makes an excellent 'instant' sauce – very 'Lazy Cook'.*

Trout Fillets with fresh Strawberries and Thyme

to serve 4
4 whole trout fillets
8 large strawberries
freshly ground white pepper
balsamic vinegar
150ml (¼pt) white wine
a few chives
several pinches fresh thyme

Set oven at gas 6/450°f/220°c/Aga roasting oven.

Put a sliced strawberry down one side of each fillet, season with pepper and a sprinkling of balsamic vinegar before covering with the other side. Put a film of the wine in an oven proof dish and add the prepared fillets. Cover with foil and bake in the pre-set oven for 10-15mins. or until the fillets are firm to the touch. Remove from the oven and place on a serving dish, or individual plates, and cover to keep warm. To the pan juices add the remaining wine, thyme and a few dashes of balsamic vinegar and boil to reduce then pour it around the fillets. Partly slice the remaining strawberries (with stalks on), so that they can be opened into a fan shape and place one on each fillet then tuck strips of chive under the strawberries – to look like sun-rays! Serve with new potatoes and a green vegetable or salad.

Lazy Cook tips –this is a delicious and colourful way of serving trout fillets. If you are feeling really extravagant bake the fillets in Champagne rather than wine (a useful way of using up half full bottles after a party). Always remember undercooked fish is inedible, overcooked fish is a disaster – the texture of the trout should be firm but moist. If they are to be served cold remember they will continue to cook as they cool.

Tuna Steaks with a Spicy Cream Sauce

to serve 4.
4 tuna steaks
a little oil
freshly ground pepper
spicy cream sauce (recipe page 29)

Heat a large frying or sauté pan. Brush the steaks on each side with oil and season with a little freshly ground pepper. Cook in the hot pan for 2mins. on each side. To serve, place the cooked steaks down the centre of a hot serving dish and drizzle with a little of the sauce, (or serve on individual plates). Serve the remaining sauce separately

Lazy Cook tips – it is important not to overcook tuna as it becomes very dry and loses its delicate flavour. This recipe is made so quickly that it is important that the sauce and any salad or vegetables to accompany it are prepared before the tuna is cooked. Served hot or cold.

Spicy Cream Sauce

1 bottle brown sauce
single cream

Whisk cream into the sauce until it is the desired flavour.   Serve hot or cold.

ICINGS/JELLIES/SYRUPS

ICINGS

Lemon – *recipe page 8.*

Savoury – *recipe page 106.*

Water – *recipe page 74.*

JELLY

Savoury – *recipe page 23.*

SYRUP

Sugar – *recipe page 70.*

MEAT and POULTRY

Chicken Breasts with Bacon Strips and Cherry Tomatoes

to serve 4
4 chicken breasts
1 tbls. plain flour
freshly ground black pepper
1-2 tbls. oil or chicken fat
4 slices thick cut bacon – cut into strips
4 spring onions – cut into short lengths
150ml (¼pt) white wine
20 cherry tomatoes
a handful of fresh basil leaves

Set oven at gas 4/400°f/1200°c/Aga baking oven.
Season the flour with freshly ground black pepper.   Heat a tablespoon of oil in a pan, lightly coat each chicken breast in the seasoned flour, add to the hot pan and cook on each side until brown (about a minute), remove from pan.   If the pan is very dry add another tablespoon of oil and when hot add the bacon strips and cook for about a minute moving them around the pan, remove from the pan.   Scrape the base of the pan to loosen any sediment and add approx. 50ml. (2fl.oz) warm water and the wine, bring to a boil and boil (without lid), to reduce a little. Add the chicken breasts, the bacon and the spring onions, bring to a simmer, cover and bake in the pre-set oven for 15-20mins. or until the chicken breasts are tender, stir in the tomatoes and some of the basil half way through cooking. Serve from the pan, or arrange the breasts down the centre of a hot serving dish, spoon the remaining ingredients on and around and scatter with the remaining basil leaves.

Lazy Cook tips – this is a very colourful dish with lots of summer flavours. It can be completely cooked on the hob as follows – when the chicken breasts and other ingredients are returned to the pan, bring it to a 'gentle' simmer, place lid on pan (or cover with foil) and simmer gently until the chicken is tender, it is important not to let it boil.   Serve with new potatoes and summer vegetables.

Jubilee Chicken – *a splendid recipe to be served on any occasion and particularly at a Jubilee Party*

to serve 8
8 chicken breasts
2 tbls. plain flour
freshly ground white pepper
1-2 tbls. oil, or chicken fat
1 large onion – skin and finely chop
300ml (½pt) white wine
150ml (¼pt) chicken stock
1 desst. Dijon mustard
1 teas. dried tarragon
a few French tarragon leaves
2 tbls. double cream

Set oven at gas 4/400°f/200°c/Aga baking oven.
Season the flour with freshly ground white pepper. Heat a tablespoon of oil in a pan. Lightly coat each chicken breast in the seasoned flour, add to the hot oil and cook on each side until brown (about a minute), remove from pan. Add a little warm water to the pan and scrape up any residue from the base before adding the prepared onion, place lid on pan and cook until the onion begins to soften. Add the wine and stock and boil for about a minute to reduce. Stir in the Dijon, tarragon and cream, add the chicken breasts and bring to a simmer, cover and put in the pre-set oven and bake for 20-30mins. or until the chicken breasts are tender. Remove from oven and leave until cold. To serve hot or cold, place the chicken breasts down the centre of a serving dish, cover with the sauce and scatter with fresh tarragon leaves. This recipe is best prepared in advance and stored, covered, in a refrigerator until needed – serve within 3 days.

Lazy Cook tips – *this recipe is best prepared in advance to allow the flavours to develop. If it is to be served to a crowd, I recommend it is prepared as on page 33.*

to serve 10-12 people (or more) –

Roast a whole chicken (2kg (5 lbs) in weight with a good quantity of French tarragon tucked into the cavity. When cold remove all the meat and break into mouth-sized pieces. Make up a double quantity of the sauce following the main recipe from the softening of the onion stage and when cold stir in the chicken pieces. Prepare it a day before it is to be served and store, covered, in a refrigerator.

Lazy Cook tips – if this is made in quantity (perhaps to serve 50 plus portions), I recommend it is stored in polythene bags to save space in the refrigerator.

Chicken Millefeuille

to serve 6-8
250gms. (8ozs) ready rolled puff pastry
500gms. (1 lb) cooked chicken
mayonnaise (recipe page 26)
fresh lemon juice
1-2tbls. freshly chopped parsley
lemon slices

Set oven at gas 7/475°f/230°c/Aga roasting oven.
Cut the pastry into two pieces, place on a wet baking tray, prick all over with a fork and bake in the pre-set oven for 8-10mins. or until the pastry has risen and is brown on top. Turn the pastry over and bake for a further 5-10mins or until cooked. Remove from oven and cool on a wire tray. To assemble, put one piece of cooked pastry on to a serving dish (or a tray covered with foil). Break the chicken into mouth-sized pieces and stir into several tablespoons of mayonnaise, with a good sprinkling of lemon juice and chopped parsley. Spread on to the pastry and top with the second piece. Garnish with lemon slices and slice to serve.

Lazy Cook tips – ready-made and rolled puff pastry can be purchased from supermarkets, fresh or frozen. Always keep some in a freezer and follow the directions on the packet for thawing and baking. Although there is no substitute in my mind for home-made mayonnaise, in a real emergency a good quality bought one can be used.

Chicken Thighs with Fresh Coriander and Bacon

to serve 4
8 boned chicken thighs
fresh coriander
8 bacon slices – without rind
150ml (¼) white wine
150ml (¼pt) chicken stock
2 tbls. single cream

Set oven at gas 6/450°f/220°c/Aga roasting oven.
Unroll each thigh and cover with fresh coriander, re-roll before covering with a rasher of bacon. Moisten the base of a shallow ovenproof dish with white wine, add the prepared thighs and bake in the pre-set oven for 15-20mins. then remove from pan and keep warm. To the pan juices add the remaining wine and stock and boil to reduce, stir in the cream and a handful of fresh coriander leaves. To serve, pile the thighs on to a hot serving dish and serve the sauce separately.

Lazy Cook tips *– if you do not have any chicken stock use all wine. When placing in the cooking dish, pack them fairly close together with the end of the bacon underneath, this way they will retain their shape. Single, whipping or double cream can be added. Chicken thighs are juicy and sweet and the combined flavours are excellent – if available, pick the coriander straight from your garden, it's easily grown and the flavour is superior to any you can buy.*

Ham and Bacon joints

A ham or bacon joint is always a useful ingredient to have in store. They can be purchased with a shelf life of several weeks and once cooked they can be stored in a fridge for 5-7 days in readiness for serving hot or cold. Bacon joints are cheaper than ham or gammon but to me the flavour is better. Although it is not fashionable to eat fat, it is the fat which contributes to the flavour – enjoy it - in small quantities. But before giving some recipes, this is how I cook these joints.

To cook a ham or bacon joint

1 ham or bacon joint
1 tbls. demerara sugar
2 dried bay leaves
10 whole cloves
10 black peppercorns

Put the joint into a large pan, cover with cold water and leave to soak for 1-2 hours. Strain off the water and discard. Cover the joint with fresh cold water and place over a 'low' heat, without lid. Bring 'slowly' to a 'gentle' simmer (an occasional bubble). Skim the top before adding the remaining ingredients, put lid on pan and continue 'gently' simmering for 30mins to 1 hour, depending on the size of the joint (this can be done in the simmering oven of an Aga). Remove from heat and leave the joint in the water (this is now stock), for 20mins. before slicing to serve hot. To serve cold, remove from the pan and when cold store, covered, in a refrigerator or cold larder.

Lazy Cook tips – I cannot over-emphasise the importance of allowing the joint to 'gently simmer' throughout cooking. The initial bringing to a 'gentle' simmer can take as long as 2hrs depending on the size of the joint – this is to allow the heat to penetrate to the centre of the joint. A good assessment of the length of time to cook the joint, once simmering point has been reached, is to allow 20mins. to each 500gms (1 lb). The stock has many uses, store it in the refrigerator or freeze it in polythene bags of varying sizes.

Ham or Bacon with Broad Beans and Fresh Coriander

to serve 4
1 kg (2lbs) broad beans
500gms (1 lb) cooked ham or bacon – cut into strips
a little single cream
a handful fresh coriander leaves

Cook the beans in a little boiling water then remove with a slotted spoon. Reduce the liquid to approximately 2fl.ozs, add the strips of ham and bring to a simmer then add the cooked beans, a little cream and finally stir in the coriander leaves. Serve hot on a bed of rice or pasta or cold on a bed of mixed salad.

Ham with a Mediterranean Sauce

to serve 4
500gms (1 lb) ham or bacon joint
mediterranean sauce (recipe below)

Cook the joint as directed on page 35. Make the sauce. To serve, remove the ham from the stock, cut it into slices and arrange down the centre of a hot serving dish, or individual plates. Drizzle with a little of the sauce and serve the remainder separately.

Lazy Cook tips – this recipe can also be served cold

Mediterranean Sauce

150ml (¼pt) ham or bacon stock
3fl.ozs salt-free vegetable stock, or water
2 teas. sundried tomato purée
3 teas. redcurrant jelly
125gms (4ozs) pitted black olives
1 square bitter chocolate

Bring the stock and water to a boil. Whisk in the tomato purée and redcurrant jelly and when they have dissolved add the olives and bring to a simmer, cover and simmer for 5mins. Before serving, whisk in the chocolate and bring back to a simmer.

Lazy Cook tips – the final simmering can be done in an Aga simmering oven. This sauce can be served hot or cold – store, covered, in a refrigerator or cold larder. I like to serve it with pasta or rice, and a green side salad for a really quick meal – very tasty and very 'Lazy Cook'!

Bacon and Parsley Sauce

to serve 4
500gms (1 lb) bacon joint
parsley sauce (recipe below)

Cook the joint as directed on page 35. Make the sauce. To serve, remove the joint from the stock, cut into slices and arrange down the centre of a to a hot serving dish, or individual plates. Serve the sauce separately.

Parsley Sauce

25gms (1 oz) butter
25gms (1 oz) plain flour
300ml. (½pt) milk
150ml. (¼pt) stock – fish, meat or vegetable
2 tbls. chopped fresh parsley
2 tbls. single cream
freshly ground white pepper

Melt the butter in a large saucepan, add the flour and mix to a paste (this is known as a 'roux'), before adding the milk and stock. Stir continuously until the mixture simmers and thickens. Stir in the parsley and cook for a minute before stirring in the cream and seasoning with freshly ground pepper. Serve immediately.

Lazy Cook tips – this is one of the few 'roux' based sauces I cook nowadays. I recommend the butter is melted, but not hot and bubbling, before the flour is added. This will ensure a smooth paste (roux) which, when all the liquid ingredients are added, can be brought to a boil and thickened. If lumps should occur, remove the pan from the heat and whisk until they dissolve. When serving this recipe with bacon or ham joints, I recommend the stock from the cooked joint is added. I prefer this sauce to be green in colour and of a runny consistency so that it lightly coats rather than hangs like a heavy blanket over the ingredients it is accompanying.

Ham Platter for a Buffet Table

to serve 25 or more people
15 eggs – boiled for 7-8mins.
freshly grated orange zest
30 slices of ham (cut not too thinly)
30 chipolata sausages - cooked
1 box mustard cress

Remove the shells and cut each egg in half lengthways before piling them (cut side up), into the centre of a very large serving dish (or tray covered with foil), and scatter with grated orange zest. Arrange the ham slices, slightly overlapping, around the eggs and tuck a cold cooked chipolata to protrude between each ham slice. Scatter with mustard cress before serving.

***Lazy Cook tips** – when catering for a crowd I buy ready cooked ham sliced not too thinly – allow one slice per person plus a few extras. For good presentation use the largest serving dish, or meat plate you possess, if necessary divide it between two dishes. The eggs can be boiled the day before but do not shell them until they are needed. The chipolatas can also be cooked a day or two in advance, they should also be stored in a refrigerator or cold larder. The combined flavours are excellent and the presentation is colourful and eye-catching.*

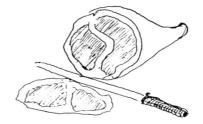

Lamb Cutlets with a Quick Tomato Sauce

to serve 4
8 lamb cutlets
1 egg
50gms (2ozs) bread – brown or white
50gms (2ozs) cooked ham – without fat
25gms (1oz) lamb dripping or 1 tbls. oil
cutlet frills
quick tomato sauce (recipe below)
garnish -
watercress

Trim any excess fat, and flatten each cutlet with a wooden rolling pin or meat hammer. Whisk the egg on a tin plate (or a shallow dish). Put the bread, including crusts, into a food processor or liquidiser and process until a breadcrumb texture, add the ham broken into pieces and process for a few seconds, remove from processor and put on to a piece of greaseproof or foil. Coat each cutlet in egg then in the breadcrumb mixture pressing this into the cutlets. Heat the dripping or oil in a large frying or sauté pan, add the prepared cutlets and brown on each side for about a minute to seal. Reduce the heat a little and continue to cook for 5-10mins. depending on how pink you wish to serve the cutlets. To serve, remove from the pan and drain on kitchen roll before topping with a cutlet frill and arranging, slightly overlapping, on a large hot dish or individual serving plates. Garnish with watercress and serve the sauce separately.

***Lazy Cook tips** – if you cook by Aga the final cooking process, after browning, can be done in the oven, make the sauce during this time and reheat to serve. These cutlets can be served hot or cold – they are excellent included in a picnic. Store, covered, in a refrigerator or cold larder. Use within 4 days.*

Quick Tomato Sauce

Heat a quantity of bottled tomato ketchup/sauce with a few shakes of Worcestershire sauce, tabasco, fresh lemon juice and a little runny honey if the flavour is too sharp. When all ingredients have blended together add a few mixed, chopped herbs Serve hot or cold. Store in a jar in a refrigerator. Use within 4 days.

Lamb Fillets with Redcurrants and Garden Mint

to serve 4
4 lamb fillets
1 tbls. plain flour seasoned with freshly ground white pepper and chopped mint
15gms (½oz) lamb dripping or a little oil
150ml. (¼pt) stock
150ml. (¼pt) red Martini
1 teas. mint jelly
250gms (8 ozs) fresh redcurrants
1 teas. fresh garden mint – roughly chopped
2 tbls. cream – single, whipping or double

Set oven at gas 6/450°f/220°c/Aga roasting oven.Dry each fillet on kitchen roll and trim off any excess fat. Heat a shallow pan and smear the base with dripping (or add a dessertspoon of oil). Lightly coat each fillet in seasoned flour, add to the hot pan, reduce the heat a little, and brown for approximately 2mins. on each side. Put, uncovered, into the pre-set oven and bake for 15-20mins. Remove the fillets and cover with foil to keep warm. Remove all excess fat from the pan, add a little stock and scrape up any sediment. Add the remaining stock and Martini and boil until it has reduced by half then whisk in the mint jelly. Reserve 4 sprigs of the redcurrants on stalks, and add the remainder, without stalks, the chopped mint and the cream and bring to a simmer. To serve, slice partly through each fillet and arrange like a fan on to one large, or individual hot serving plates. Place a sprig of redcurrants on each and pour the sauce around.

Lazy Cook tips *– the length of cooking time depends on how pink you wish to serve the fillets. If fresh fillets are not available frozen ones are an excellent buy – keep some in the freezer.*

Lamb with Orange and Rosemary and a Brandy Sauce

to serve 4
1 loin of lamb, a minimum of 8 cutlets – chined (see *Lazy Cook* tips)
2 fresh oranges
several sprigs fresh rosemary
300ml (½) stock
6 tbls. brandy
3 tbls. double cream
cutlet frills
1 bunch watercress

Set oven at gas 6/450°f/220°c/Aga roasting oven.
Trim any excess fat from the loin and cut partway through each cutlet. Cut 8 thin orange slices, including the peel, fold round a sprig of fresh rosemary and tuck into the cut between each cutlet, skin side out and at the meaty end.   Stand the prepared loin on a trivet in a roasting tin and pour in a little hot water to cover the base.   Squeeze the juice from the remaining oranges over the loin and bake in the pre-set oven for 20-30mins. depending on how pink you wish the meat to be served.   When cooked to your liking remove from oven and place on a hot serving dish and cover loosely with foil to keep warm.   Spoon excess fat from the roasting tin and scrape up any sediment from the base.   Add the stock and brandy and boil until it has reduced by half. Stir in the cream and bring to a simmer before pouring into a hot sauce boat.   Before serving, put a cutlet frill on each cutlet and garnish with watercress.   Serve with new minted potatoes and garden peas or mangetout to complete the flavours.

Lazy Cook tips – it is important to make sure the loin has been chined so that individual cutlets can be cut, ask your butcher to do this.   Allow 2 cutlets per person, and 2 extra.   Two loins may be needed to serve more than 4 people.   Reduce the oven temperature after 20mins. cooking to gas 4/400°f/200°c/Aga baking oven.   A prime joint, served in splendour!

Summer Liver

to serve 4
500gms (1 lb) lambs liver – thinly sliced
1 tbls. plain flour seasoned with freshly ground black pepper
25gms. (1oz) lambs dripping or 1 tbls. oil
2 lemons fresh parsley – chopped

Heat the dripping or oil in a large frying or sauté pan. Dry each liver slice on kitchen roll before lightly coating in seasoned flour. Cook in the hot fat turning it over when blood seeps out. Remove from the pan and arrange on a serving plate, slightly overlapping. Sprinkle with lemon juice and scatter with grated lemon zest and chopped parsley. Serve when cold.

Lazy Cook tips – buy lambs or calves liver for this recipe. Served with a green salad and fresh bread this is one of my favourite summer lunches. It can be made and stored, covered, in a refrigerator or cold larder, until required, bring it back to room temperature before serving. Use within 5 days. Add a little stock or water to the pan, scrape up the sediment from the base, bring to the boil then pour into a pot. When cold store it in a refrigerator and use it in meat soups and sauces - remove the fat which will have set on the top before using.

Pork Fillet with a Burnt Pepper Sauce

To serve 4
1 large pork fillet
a little flour seasoned with freshly ground pepper
1 tbls. oil
burnt pepper sauce (recipe page 44)

Set oven at gas 6/450°f/220°c/Aga roasting oven.
Cut the fillet in half and lightly coat each in seasoned flour. Heat the oil in a pan, add the prepared fillets and brown. Put into the pre-set oven and bake for 20-30mins. or until they are cooked, reducing the oven temperature after 10mins. to gas 4/400°f/ 200°c/Aga baking oven. When cooked, remove from oven and allow to rest for 10mins. before slicing. To serve, arrange the slices down a large serving dish, or on individual plates, and pour a little of the sauce over, serve the remainder separately.

***Lazy Cook tips** – test that the pork is cooked by piercing the thickest part with a metal skewer, it is cooked when the juices run clear. The fillet can be cooked whole if you prefer.*

Burnt Pepper Sauce

to serve 4
2 red peppers
1 tbls. oil
6 small mushrooms
3 ozs orange juice (from a carton)
thyme

Set oven at gas 6/400°f/200°c/Aga roasting oven.

Cut each pepper into quarters and remove all seeds and any white flesh. Wipe the mushrooms with damp kitchen paper. Brush the pepper skins and the mushroom tops with oil and place in a lightly oiled ovenproof dish (skin side up) and put in the pre-set oven for 10mins. Remove the mushrooms and continue baking the peppers until the skins begin to burn. Remove from oven and put the peppers and mushrooms into a liquidiser or processor and mix to a purée. Stir the orange juice into the baking dish and scrape up all residue, add the purée and a several good pinches of thyme, bring to a simmer then serve.

Lazy Cook tips – the peppers and mushrooms can be browned under a grill if you prefer. Choose a baking dish which can be used on the hob and in the oven. A sauce with lots of flavour and rich colour in colour.

Pork Steaks with fresh Peach Halves and a hint of Sage

to serve 4
4 pork steaks
a little flour seasoned with freshly ground pepper and 1 teas. sage
1 tbls. oil
4 peaches – cut in half and remove stones
25gms (1oz) butter
150ml (¼pt) stock

Set oven at gas 4/400°f/200°c/Aga baking oven.

Trim all excess fat from the steaks then coat them lightly in the seasoned flour. Heat the oil, add the prepared steaks and brown on each side, remove from pan. Add the butter to the pan and when melted add the peach halves (cut side down), and cook until they begin to brown, remove and drain off all excess fat from the pan before adding the stock, scrape up all residue from the base of the pan and bring the stock to the boil. Return the steaks and the peaches (cut side up), bring to a simmer, cover and bake in the pre-set oven for 30-40mins. or until the steaks are tender. Serve on one large serving dish, or individual plates.

Lazy Cook tips – I buy shoulder steaks for this recipe. If dried sage is used reduce the quantity added to the flour by half.

Pork Terrine

to serve 8
225gms (8ozs) diced pork
225gms (8ozs) pork sausages – remove skins
225gms (8ozs) lambs liver – cut up
175gms (6ozs) dried prunes – without stones
2 tbls. fresh breadcrumbs – brown or white
fresh sage
freshly ground white pepper
100ml. (4fl.oz) approx. red wine
bay leaf

Mix the pork, sausages and liver together using a fork.   Add the remaining ingredients (except the bay leaf) and stir well.   Leave for about one hour before packing into a terrine dish.   Place a bay leaf in the centre, cover with a lid or foil, and stand the dish in a pan with warm water to come half way up the dish. Bake at gas 3/300°f/ 150°c/Aga simmering oven for about one hour or until firm to the touch   Remove the dish from the water and leave to cool.   Store in a fridge.   Use within 7 days.

Lazy Cook tips – make in one large or several small dishes, or ramekins. Baking in a water bath (bain-marie) ensures even cooking throughout.   A terrine is a very useful ingredient to have in store, serve it with salad and bread or with a platter of cold meats or poultry – a good 'stretching' ingredient when unexpected guests arrive!

Turkey and Mushroom Terrine

to serve 8 slices
10-12 rashers streaky bacon (without rind) – stretch with a knife
1 teas. dried parsley
6 turkey breast steaks
4-6 medium sized flat mushrooms – wipe with damp kitchen paper
– remove stalks
freshly ground white pepper
parsley and thyme stuffing (recipe page 47)

Set oven at gas 6/450°f/220°c/Aga roasting oven.
Lightly oil a 900gm. (2 lb) loaf tin. Make a trellis pattern in the tin by putting rashers of bacon down the centre of the base and ends of the tin with some overhanging each end. Put more bacon rashers down the sides and base, spaced roughly 2cms. (1") apart. Sprinkle a little dried parsley in the empty squares on the base of the tin. Put a layer of turkey steaks to cover the base then cover with half the stuffing. Put a line of mushrooms on top of the stuffing, (skin side uppermost), and cover with the remaining stuffing. Cover with the remaining steaks and any overlapping bacon and press down with your hand. Cover with buttered greaseproof and seal with foil. Stand the tin on a baking tray and bake in the pre-set oven for 10mins. before reducing the temperature to gas 4/400°f/200°c/Aga baking oven and continue baking for 30-40mins. or until the turkey is firm to the touch. Loosen the foil and, wearing an oven glove, press down on the ingredients then place a heavy weight on top. Leave in the tin for 10mins. before loosening the sides with a palette knife and turning on to a hot serving dish. Slice to serve, hot or cold, as a main course, or a light meal, or starter. I like to serve this with Spicy Cream Sauce (recipe page 29).

Lazy Cook tips – the trellis pattern made by the bacon gives this terrine a nice summer presentation. If it is to be served cold leave it, weighted, in the baking tin for 30mins. Remove from tin, and when cold, wrap in greaseproof and foil and store in a refrigerator until needed. Bring back to room temperature to serve. Heavy tins or jars can be used as weights.

Parsley and Thyme Stuffing

175gms (6 ozs) fresh breadcrumbs (brown or white)
a handful of fresh parsley
a handful of fresh thyme
1 egg
zest of 1 lemon
2 tbls. fresh lemon juice
freshly ground white pepper

Break the bread into pieces and put into a food processor or liquidiser with the parsley and thyme and process until a breadcrumb texture. Add all remaining ingredients and process to a sticky paste. Spread into a lightly oiled ovenproof dish, or shape into rounds and place on a lightly oiled ovenproof dish. Allow to rest for 15mins. before baking at gas 4/400°f/200°c/Aga baking oven for 10-15mins. Serve hot or cold.

Lazy Cook tips – *a useful stuffing to serve especially with poultry. If using dried herbs, add 1 teas. of each. When making this to add to the Turkey and Mushroom Terrine (recipe page 46), process the mushrooms stalks with the ingredients.*

PASTA AND RICE

Pasta and rice have wonderful 'stretching' qualities - with the addition of a handful of ingredients, and a simple sauce they can be made to feed a few or a crowd. I chose to serve 'Pasta with Summer Vegetables and a Mediterranean Sauce' (recipe page 51) at an impromptu party I arranged on the day of my husband's 60th birthday. You can read about this on page 50.

PASTA

Pasta with Chicken and Fresh Apricots and Lemon Balm

to serve 4-6
340gm pkt mini chicken breast fillets
1 tbls. plain flour seasoned with freshly ground white pepper
1 tbls. oil
250gms (8ozs) fresh apricots – stone and cut into quarters
1 lemon
1 medium onion – skin and cut into rings
100ml (4ozs) chicken stock (or a mixture of stock and white wine)
1 tbls. fresh lemon balm - chopped
250gms (8ozs) pasta shapes – cook as directed on packet

Set oven at gas 4/400°f/200°c/Aga baking oven.
Lightly coat the chicken fillets in the seasoned flour and brown lightly in the hot oil, put into the pre-set oven and bake until tender. Simmer the apricots for 2-3mins. in approx. 100ml (4ozs) water with a few strips of lemon rind (lid on pan). Strain off the juice and reserve, discard the lemon rind. Remove the cooked fillets from the pan and keep warm. Add a little of the reserved apricot juice to the pan and scrape up any sediment from the base before adding the prepared onions and cook until they begin to soften (lid on pan). Remove the onions, pour the stock, the remainder of the apricot juices and a good squeeze of lemon juice into the pan and boil until reduced a little. Return the fillets and onion, the cooked pasta and the lemon balm to the pan and stir over a gentle heat for a few minutes. Pile on to a hot serving dish, or individual dishes, and serve.

Lazy Cook tips - *test that the chicken fillets are cooked by piercing with a skewer, they are cooked when the juices run clear. Adding a little liquid to the pan will soften any bits sticking to the base and they will be more easily scraped up.*

Pasta with Chicken Livers

to serve 4-6
1 tbls. oil
25gms (1oz) butter
250gms (8ozs) chicken livers
2 medium onions – skin and slice into rings
1 teas. fresh rosemary
2 teas. grain mustard
freshly ground black pepper
300ml (½pt) white wine (or a mixture of wine and stock)
50ml. (2 fl.ozs) single cream
250gms (8 ozs) pasta shapes – cook as directed on the packet
100gms (4ozs) parmesan cheese – grated or shavings

Heat the oil, add the butter and when melted add the chicken livers and the lemon juice and cook for a minute or two, stirring occasionally. Remove the livers from the pan and keep warm. Add a little water to the pan and scrape up the sediment from the base before adding the onion rings, place lid on pan and cook until the onions begin to soften remove from pan. Add the wine and boil to reduce by half. Stir in the rosemary, mustard and cream, season with freshly ground pepper and bring to a simmer. Add the cooked livers and the juices which will have seeped out, the onion and the cooked pasta, stir well and bring back to a simmer before serving piled into hot individual serving dishes or one large serving dish. Serve grated or shavings of parmesan separately.

Lazy Cook tips – make this in a sauté or large pan. You will find it is much easier to scrape the sediment from the base of the pan if a little liquid is added.

PIMM'S AND PASTA PARTY

The sky was overcast but not threatening.   It was the morning of my husband's 60th birthday. A family party was arranged for the weekend but I decided we should celebrate today.   Out of earshot of the birthday boy I telephoned friends from in and around the village and invited them to come for Pimm's and Pasta at 6 o'clock.

Over elevenses I made a shopping list and before lunch drove into Stroud and bought all the ingredients I needed to serve Pasta with Summer Vegetables and a Mediterranean Sauce, to 40 friends.   After lunch I listened to The Archers, had a little read and then went for a walk before deciding to make a start on the pasta. Knowing only too well that, however simple the recipe, it takes longer to prepare a meal for 40 than it does for 4 and I soon realised I had been a little too relaxed about the time, and I should have made an earlier start.   In addition to the pasta there was the Pimm's to be made and the garden to be set with additional chairs and tables.

By 5p.m. I began to panic just a fraction at which point my husband strolled into the kitchen. "Are you making jam" he asked, noticing the preserving pan on the table full to the brim with colourful ingredients. "No, it's supper" I answered. "Supper! - isn't there rather a lot for two of us?" was his reply. At this point I had to tell him that it was a birthday celebration and a few friends were arriving - in an hour.   "Oh how nice, who's coming? how many people"? he enquired — "about 40" was my hastened reply as I poured the sauce into the pan full of pasta and vegetables.   I was grateful for his offer of help and together we set up the garden and made the Pimm's just in time for the first friends to arrive - only to realise, as the Pimm's was about to be poured, that Mo, not for the first time, had forgotten to borrow the necessary tumblers!   Cupboards were hastily searched and an assortment of tumblers was collected — the clouds lifted and the evening was a happy one and long to be remembered.

Pasta with Summer Vegetables in a Mediterranean Cream Sauce

to serve 4-6
250gms (8 ozs) pasta shapes – cook as instructed on packet
a selection of vegetables to include –
courgette slices
red onion rings
peppers (of various colours) - sliced
mangetout - cooked whole
baby sweetcorn – cooked whole
asparagus tips
225gms (8ozs) seedless grapes
mediterranean cream sauce (recipe below)
100gms (4ozs) parmesan cheese – grated or shavings

Cook the prepared vegetables in 300ml (½pt) boiling water until they begin to soften, lid on pan. Strain through a colander and rinse under a cold running tap. Add to the cooked pasta and the sauce and mix together before serving. Serve grated or shavings of parmesan separately.

Lazy Cook tips *– the vegetables should be crisp in texture, avoid overcooking. The vegetable stock can be stored in a fridge for future use. I prefer pasta twists to other shapes. This is an ideal recipe to serve at a Pimm's and Pasta party.*

Mediterranean Cream Sauce

300ml (½pt) white wine – boil to reduce by half
1 teas. sundried tomato purée
6 sundried tomatoes preserved in oil – slice
100gms. (4ozs) pitted black olives
1 tbls. mixed fresh herbs – chopped
1 teas. balsamic or wine vinegar
freshly ground white pepper
50ml. (2ozs) single cream

Whisk the tomato purée into the reduced wine before adding all the remaining ingredients. Stir well before serving.

Lazy Cook tips – *make in advance and store, in a covered jar or jug in a refrigerator. Stir well before using. Use within 5 days. A good sauce to serve, hot or cold, with pasta and rice dishes. This quantity is sufficient for the Pasta with Summer Vegetables in a Mediterranean Cream Sauce (recipe page 51).*

RICE

Summer Savoury Rice

to serve 4-6
2 x 125gm sachets Camargue red rice (cook as instructed on the packet)
350gms (12ozs) cooked chicken – cut into small pieces
½ a ring of black pudding – remove skin
2 spring onions – cut into short lengths
8 fresh apricots –cut into slices
handful of seedless grapes
good tbls. fresh mixed herbs – chopped
8 sundried tomatoes in oil – drain from oil and cut into strips
2 handfuls celery – cut into small pieces
few twists freshly ground black pepper
150ml (¼pt) single cream
2 teas. whole grain mustard
1 avocado

With the exception of the avocado, mix all the ingredients into the rice and pile on to a serving dish. Cut the avocado in half using a stainless steel knife, remove the centre stone and peel each half before cutting into slices, arrange these in a circle in the centre of the rice, slightly overlapping.

Lazy Cook tips – *always use a stainless steel knife when cutting an avocado and it should not discolour. We belong to a local Theatre Club and I often take this to eat on the coach – pack it into individual dishes. It helps if you remember to take a spoon to eat it with! My recipe for cooking rice can be found on page 53.*

To cook rice

250 gms (8ozs) quantity

Put the rice into a sieve and wash under a cold running tap before adding to a pan containing 1ltr. (2pts) boiling water, stir well, bring to a simmer, put lid on pan and simmer gently for 20-30mins. or until the rice is of a nutty texture. Pour back into a sieve and rinse thoroughly under a cold running tap, drain well. The cooked grains should remain whole, tender and separate. Use or store, covered, in a fridge or cold larder. Use within 3 days.

PRESERVES

Chutneys / Jams / Vinegars

I'm not so lazy a cook that I cannot spend a little time making 'small' quantities of jams and chutneys even if it is only with the idea of entering them into the Bisley Flower Show in the hope of winning a prize!   But before giving a few of my favourite recipes I thought you might enjoy hearing about one of my early experiences of fruit picking ....

FRUIT PICKING

Shortly after our move to Bisley and during a visit from my mother-in-law, I decided we should all go fruit picking with the intention of making jam.

It was a hot summer's morning and we decided to motor to Newent from where I was told the best fruit could be picked.   Mother-in-law and I set out armed with sun hats, drinks and three small children, all very excited at the prospect of this new adventure.   It had been my intention to pick strawberries only in the hope that a much needed touch of magic might be added to my attempts at this particular jam, my previous efforts having resulted in a dark strawberry syrup.   To my surprise, when we arrived at the farm there were strawberries, raspberries, loganberries, gooseberries, red and black currants, all awaiting our eager picking fingers.   We all ate and picked, in that order, our silent concentration being interrupted only by the occasional cries of "I've never seen such a big strawberry in my whole life" from one of my sons then all of four years old!

We started the homeward journey with my little car packed to capacity with baskets of fruit of all kinds, three weary children and an equally exhausted Mother-in-law. Stopping at a grocer's shop for ice-creams I discovered there was a sudden sugar shortage. "Sugar is likely to become rationed" stated the excited shopkeeper. That was all I needed to hear. On arriving home I realised my preserving pan was far too small for such large quantities of fruit and after much telephoning around the village a neighbour came to my rescue and loaned me her beautiful new, large preserving pan, which I promptly burnt the base of.

It was an unusually hot summer and the picked fruit was deteriorating by the minute in the garage. I had no freezer and I was soon to discover I had precious few empty jam jars either. More telephone calls were made around the village and notices placed in the windows of the village shops and post office urgently requesting jam pots of any size. The whole village by now must have been wondering about this mad cook who had arrived in their midst.

Between telephone calls I had yet another abortive attempt at making strawberry jam and vowed I would never again waste time and ingredients on a luxury which was clearly beyond my ability. Eventually grateful neighbours shared most of our crop and the remainder we ate and enjoyed and then forgot about, until the next jam season.

CHUTNEY

Damson Chutney

yield approx. 4 x 350ml. (12oz) jars
900gms (2lbs) damsons
500gms (1 lb) onions – skin and chop
250gms (8 ozs) pitted dates – cut up
500gms (1 lb) raisins
500gms (1 lb) dark cane sugar
900ml (1½pts) spiced vinegar

Remove the stalks and wash the damsons, then break the skin of each fruit by cutting with a pointed knife before putting with remaining ingredients into a preserving or large, heavy based pan and stir. Bring slowly to the boil (without lid), stirring occasionally. Reduce to a 'gentle' simmer and continue until the ingredients have reduced considerably and have thickened (this can take up to 2hrs). Take the pan from the heat and remove the damson stones which will have risen to the surface. Pot into clean, hot jars, cover with a disc of greaseproof and a lid. Label and store in a cold dry place. Store for 3 months before serving.

Lazy Cook tips - the long slow cooking period is important during which time the ingredients need only the occasional stir. Once the initial boiling point is reached the heat should be reduced so that the ingredients 'gently' simmer (occasional bubbles). Test the flavour during the gentle simmering period, if it is too sharp stir in a little more sugar. Do not fill the jars to the top if metal lids are added, the vinegar will corrode the lids. Chutney is best made and stored for a few months before serving during which time the flavour will improve considerably. The damson season is a short one – buy, wash and freeze them until you have time to make into chutney, defrost them before cooking. This is my favourite of all chutneys.

Plum Chutney
Follow the recipe and Lazy Cook tips for Damson Chutney (recipe above) substituting plums for damsons.

JAM MAKING

Things to remember -

It is important to use a heavy based pan at least double the size of the quantity of fruit because rapidly boiling jam rises in the pan - watch carefully during this process.

Soft fruits i.e. strawberries and raspberries are low in pectin and little or no water need be added whereas firmer fruits i.e. plums and damsons will set even when water is added and these are more economical jams to make.

I recommend "pectin" sugar is added when preserving soft fruits which are low in pectin, and "granulated" or "preserving" sugar for plums and damsons which contain more pectin.

I prefer to add less sugar than the traditional 500gms (1 lb) per 500gms (1 lb) fruit.

The sugar must be completely dissolved before the ingredients are allowed to boil. This can take 2-3 mins. continual stirring with a wooden spoon (off the heat), but it is time well spent because undissolved sugar will cause the jam to crystallise. Test that it has dissolved by prodding the base of the pan with the spoon when the jam is still.

Most summer fruits can be preserved as jam. Flavours can be varied by mixing fruits – experiment with your favourite fruits.

Always use fruit of the best quality. Don't get carried away – make small quantities.

To test for a set -

After the recommended time for 'rapid boiling', remove the pan from the heat and put a little jam on to a plate and leave until it becomes cold and a skin forms. Push a finger through the centre to make a channel and if this does not close the jam is set. If the channel closes, bring the jam back to a rapid boil and test every 2mins. until a set is reached. I prefer the consistency of jam to be not too solid and as long as the channel does not completely close I am happy to pot it.

JAM

Apricot Jam

yield approx. 4 x 350gms (12oz) jars
900gms (2 lbs) apricots – stone
175ml (6 fl.ozs) cold water
2 tbls. lemon juice
800gms (1¾lbs) pectin sugar
jam pot covers

Put the washed fruit, water and lemon juice into a preserving or large heavy based pan and cook over a low heat, without lid, until the fruit has softened and the contents of the pan are considerably reduced. ✳ Add the sugar and stir until it has completely dissolved (see 'things to remember' on page 57). Bring to boiling point and boil rapidly for 5mins. before testing for a set as described on page 57).   Once a set has been reached, allow the jam to cool a little before potting into clean, hot jars. Seal with jam pot covers and a metal lid, if available.   When cold, label and store in a cool, dry place.

Lazy Cook tips – this quantity of jam can be made in about 30mins. A preserving funnel (available from all good kitchen shops), will make the potting a much less sticky job. Jam pot covers can be purchased from all good kitchen shops and supermarkets.

Damson Jam

yield approx. 4 x 350gms (12oz) jars
900gms. (2lbs) damsons - washed
600ml. (1pt) water
700gms (1½lbs) granulated sugar
jam pot covers

Break the skin of each fruit by cutting with a pointed knife before putting it into a preserving or large heavy based pan with the water. Cook over a low heat, without lid, until the fruit has softened and the contents of the pan are considerably reduced. Continue from ✳ in Apricot Jam recipe above.

Lazy Cook tips – *remove the damson stones after setting point has been reached.*

Plum Jam

yield approx. 4 x 350gm. (12oz) jars
900gms. (2lbs) plums
600ml. (1pt) water
700gms (1½lbs) granulated sugar
jam pot covers

Wash the plums then cut in half and remove and discard the stones. Put the fruit and water into a preserving or large heavy based pan and cook over a low heat, without lid, until the fruit has softened and the contents of the pan are considerably reduced. Continue from ✶ in Apricot Jam recipe on page 58.

Lazy Cook tips – *if the stones are not easily removed leave them, they will rise to the top and can be removed after setting point has been reached. This quantity of jam can be made in about 30mins.*

Raspberry Jam

yield approx. 2 x 350gm. (12oz) jars
500gms (1 lb) raspberries
1 tbls. fresh lemon juice
350gms (12ozs) pectin sugar
jam pot covers

Cover the base of a preserving or large heavy based pan with a film of cold water. Wash the raspberries under a cold running tap, put into the pan with the lemon juice and cook over a low heat, without lid, until the fruit has softened and the contents of the pan have considerably reduced. Continue from ✶ in Apricot Jam recipe on page 58.

Lazy Cook tips – *this quantity of jam can be made in about 30mins.*

Strawberry Jam

yield approx. 2 x 350gm. (12oz) jars
500gms (1 lb) strawberries
1 tbls. fresh lemon juice
350gms (12ozs) pectin sugar
jam pot covers

Cover the base of a preserving or large heavy based pan with a film of cold water.   Remove the husks before washing the strawberries under a cold running tap, put into the pan with the lemon juice and cook over a low heat, without lid, until the fruit has softened and the contents of the pan has considerably reduced.   Continue from ✳ in Apricot Jam recipe on page 57.

Lazy Cook tips – *this quantity of jam can be made in about 30mins.*

VINEGARS

Blackberry or Raspberry Vinegar

1¼ltrs (2pts) fresh berries
1¼ltrs (2pts) white vinegar
granulated sugar

Wash and hull the berries, drain well, pour vinegar over. Leave, covered, in a refrigerator or cold larder for 4 days, stirring each morning. Strain and add 500gms (1 lb) sugar to every 600ml (1 pt) of liquid. Bring slowly to the boil, reduce to a simmer and simmer for 20mins. Bottle when cold, cork or seal tightly.

Lazy Cook tips – *this recipe was given to me by Daisy Toll, a dear friend who lived in the village for many years.*

PUDDINGS

Chocolate and Strawberry Gateau

to serve 6-8 slices
1 chocolate cake (recipe page 6)
4-6tbls Creme de Cacao (chocolate liqueur) - optional
300ml (½pt) double cream
500gms (1 lb) fresh strawberries
50gms (2ozs) bitter chocolate
icing sugar

Put the cake on to a large serving/gateau plate (or a round tray covered with foil) and pour creme de cacao into it. Whip the cream to a soft peak and spread it all over the cake. Cut the strawberries in half and them push into the cream. Melt the chocolate and trail it from a spoon over the cake and when set sift with icing sugar. Slice to serve.

Lazy Cook tips *– do not remove the husks (green leaves), from all the strawberries, they will give additional colour and interest to the gateau. Melt chocolate in a microwave or the simmering oven of an Aga.*

Crème Caramel

to serve 6
caramel (recipe page 63)
600ml. (1 pt) full cream milk
1 desst. granulated sugar
4 large eggs – whisk together
1 teas. vanilla essence
a little butter

Set oven at gas 4/400°f/200°c/Aga baking oven.

Line a warmed 900ltr (1½pt) glass or china soufflé dish with caramel by pouring the caramel from the pan into the dish and turning it until the sides and base are covered then leave to set. Make the custard by warming the milk and sugar in a pan before pouring it on to the whisked eggs. Stir in the vanilla essence and pour it, through a sieve, into the lined dish. Cover with a double thickness of buttered greaseproof and tie with string. Stand the dish in a pan and add warm water (bain marie), to come approximately half way up the dish. Bake in the pre-set oven for 10 mins. before reducing the temperature to gas 3/300°f/150°c/Aga simmering oven until the custard has set. Remove from the oven, lift out of the baking pan and leave to become cold. Serve or store in a refrigerator until needed, use within 4 days. To serve, turn on to a serving plate. Serve with single cream.

Lazy Cook tips – I always warm the dish into which the very hot caramel is to be added to prevent it (the dish) cracking. Because the caramel is so hot I hold the dish with an oven-cloth to protect my hands. I allow the caramel to become quite dark before lining the dish, almost on the point of burning, otherwise I find the pudding sweet and insipid. Turn it out on to a dish or plate with a deep rim to accommodate some of the caramel which will have dissolved into syrup. This is one of the most delicious puddings I serve.

Caramel

5 tbls. cold water
5 tbls. granulated sugar

Put the water and sugar into a small heavy based saucepan and stir over a very low heat until every grain of sugar has dissolved. Raise the heat and boil rapidly (lots of bubbles - no stirring at this point), until it turns golden or dark in colour. Remove from heat and use as directed in the recipe on page

Lazy Cook tips – watch the pan once the syrup starts to boil rapidly, it will suddenly begin to change colour. I allow it to become dark, almost on the point of burning, it takes away the sweet, syrupy flavour.

Fruit Compôte

Put an assortment of summer fruits, sliced or whole, into a pan with a little water and simmer over a gentle heat, with lid on pan, until they soften. Sweeten to taste with runny honey or sugar and serve hot, warm or cold.

Lazy Cook tips – I cannot resist buying great quantities of summer fruits and berries as they appear on the market stalls forgetting that unlike winter fruits they quickly perish. Cooked as in the above recipe (known in the family as fruit 'compost') they provide a delicious concoction to serve with or without cream or ice-cream. The flavours will vary as the season progresses. Store, when cold, covered, in a refrigerator. Remove large stones and always wash the fruit before cooking.

Gateau Royale

This gateau looks very regal decorated as suggested, but it is also equally good when assembled very simply by sandwiching the plates with whipped cream and raspberries or strawberries or a selection of fresh summer fruits.

serves 10-12
3 sponge plates (recipe page 65)
600ml (1 pt) double cream
150ml. (¼pt) full cream milk
6 peaches – each cut into 12-16 slices
6 apricots – each cut into 8-10 slices
4 nectarines – each cut into 12-16 slices
250gms (½lb) seedless white grapes
250gms (½lb) white cherries – stoned

Whip the cream and milk together to a soft peak.   Assemble directly on to a gateau plate (or a round tray covered with foil), by sandwiching the plates together with the cream and a selection of the fruits, reserving 16-20 choicest peach slices, 12 or more grapes and a cherry.   Decorate the top as follows – spread with the remaining cream and pile the grapes into the centre and encase them in 5 or 6 peach slices (like a coronet).   Put the remaining peach slices round the edge, slightly overlapping towards the centre and finally place a whole cherry on top of the coronet.   Slice to serve.

Lazy Cook tips – *it is the use of sponge plates in this recipe which makes it so special. These are not difficult to make following my 'Lazy Cook' method. They can be made and stored for several days before they are served. When summer fruits are at their best this is a delicious gateau to serve. Always wash fresh fruit before eating.*

<u>Sponge Plates</u>

makes 3 plates
3 large eggs
75gms (3ozs) caster sugar
75gms (3ozs) plain flour
a little extra caster sugar

Set oven at gas 3/300°f/150°c/Aga simmering oven.   Put the eggs and sugar into a mixer bowl, with the whisk or beaters (not plastic), and put into the oven to warm (this should take approximately 5mins.).   Remove from oven and increase the oven temperature to gas 6/450°f/220°c/Aga roasting oven.   Whisk the warmed ingredients at top speed until they are of a thick consistency (this should take approximately 5mins.) during this time oil 3 baking trays.   Sieve the flour into the thickened egg mixture and fold in, then spread it on to the prepared trays shaped like plates approximately 25cms (10") in diameter.   Scatter with caster sugar and bake in the pre-set oven for 4-5mins. or until they turn a pale biscuit colour.   Remove from oven and put immediately on to wire trays to cool (use a metal spatula to ease them off the baking trays).   If not for immediate use store them in sealed polythene bags when cold.

Lazy Cook tips – *warming the eggs and sugar is my 'Lazy Cook' answer to whisking over a bowl of hot water which seems to take an eternity during which time you are unable to prepare other ingredients.   But do watch it carefully, the eggs must not cook – you will be able to time this with practice. Plastic whisks and bowls should not be put into a hot oven. This mixture can also be shaped into sponge fingers and drops.*

Meringues

Meringue puddings are always popular and a selection of meringue shapes is a useful ingredient to have in the cupboard, they keep for months in airtight containers or polythene bags. Follow the Basic Meringue Recipe below and spread into different shapes.

Basic Meringue Recipe

the whites of 4 large eggs
250gms (8ozs) caster sugar
a pinch cream of tartar
Set oven at gas 3/300°f/220°c/Aga simmering oven.

Cover baking trays with household parchment or bake-o-glide (no need to oil). Whisk the egg whites until they are of a dry, cottonwool texture. Whisk in the sugar and cream of tartar. Spread into the required shape and dry in the pre-set oven until they will peel off the baking parchment. Store in an airtight container or in airtight polythene bags. They will remain crisp for 3 months.

Meringue Bases and Plates
Spread the basic meringue mixture into rounds in sizes varying from 5cms (2") to 25cms (10") in diameter. Dry and store as directed in the Basic Meringue recipe above.

Meringues Petites
Drop teaspoons, dessertspoons or tablespoons of the Basic Meringue mixture on to the prepared baking trays. Dry and store as directed in the Basic Meringue recipe above.

Meringue Rings
Spread into rings approximately 25cms (10") in diameter with a 7cm (3") hole in the centre. Dry and store as directed in the Basic Meringue recipe above.

Mini Raspberry Meringues

to make approx 24
12 x 6cm (2½") round meringue bases approx. 6cm (2½") in diameter
(recipe page 66)
300ml (½pt) double cream
1 tbls. raspberry syrup
500gms (1 lb) fresh raspberries

Make the meringue bases following the Basic Meringue recipe on page 66.
Whip the cream and raspberry syrup to a soft peak and sandwich half of it
between the meringue bases.   Spread the remaining cream on top and
cover with raspberries.

Lazy Cook tips *– assemble these an hour or more before serving to allow
the meringue to soften a little.   They look very pretty served individually.
This recipe can also be presented as one large meringue using larger
shaped plates.*

Praline Meringue

2 meringue plates approx. 25cms (10") in diameter (recipe page 66)
425ml (¾pt) double cream
praline powder (recipe page 68)

Whip the cream to a soft peak then fold in half the praline powder.   Place
one meringue plate on to a gateau/serving plate and spread with half the
cream, top with the second meringue, spread with the remaining cream and
scatter with the remaining praline powder.   Make several hours before
serving, slice to serve.

Lazy Cook tips *– the very first time I served this pudding to an elderly
relative, also an excellent cook, she commented she hadn't eaten anything
as good outside the 'Savoy' – I considered that praise indeed.   It is a very
delicious pudding which I'm sure will delight your guests.   With the
meringue plates and the praline made in advance, it is assembled in
minutes.   For a very special presentation the top of the meringue can be
piped with swirls of whipped cream.*

Praline Powder

caramel (recipe page 63)
50gms (2ozs) flaked almonds – browned

Make a foil case by turning up the edges of a sheet of foil (approx. 20cms/8" in size), by 2cms. (½") all round and place this on a thick pad of newspapers. Make the caramel as directed in the recipe on page 63 and when it is golden or dark brown in colour, pour it on to the foil case and leave to set hard. Break up the set caramel into pieces using a wooden rolling pin or a meat hammer then put it into a food processor or liquidiser with the browned almonds and process until it forms a crunchy powder. Store in an airtight jar. Use within 2 weeks.

Lazy Cook tips – to prevent the praline scattering all over the kitchen, cover it with a piece of greaseproof before hammering it into pieces. I devised this 'lazy cook' method of making praline powder once I realised what a useful ingredient it was; it will transform an ordinary pudding or cake into a luxury confection. It is also excellent for making chocolates.

Fresh Strawberry Meringue Ring

to serve 6
2 meringue rings (recipe page 66)
500gms (1 lb) fresh strawberries
300ml (½pt) double cream
a little icing sugar
50gms (2 ozs) bitter chocolate – melted
fresh mint leaves

Make the meringue rings following the Basic Meringue recipe on page 66. Dip the ends of 6-8 choice strawberries (with husks) in the melted chocolate and put on a wire tray to set. Put one meringue ring on to a gateau plate (or round tray covered with foil), whip the cream to a soft peak and spread half over the meringue ring. Slice the remaining strawberries and put on the cream then cover with the remaining cream. Place the second meringue ring on top and decorate with the chocolate coated strawberries. Trail any remaining chocolate, from a spoon, over the meringue before sieving with a little icing sugar.

Lazy Cook tips – *assemble this pudding at least an hour before serving, this will allow the meringue to soften and make it easier to slice.*

Nectarine and Brandy Pie

to serve 6
200gms (½lb) filo pastry
8 nectarines
2-3tbls. brandy
a little soft brown sugar – optional
25gms (1oz) melted butter
whipped cream – optional

Cut the nectarines in half and remove and discard the stones. Slice the nectarine halves into a dish and cover with a few tablespoons of brandy and leave to marinate for 30mins to 1 hr stirring occasionally. Set oven at 6/450°f/220°c/Aga roasting oven. Butter well a round tin approx. 18cms (7") in diameter and preferably with a loose base and line it with several layers of filo pastry leaving plenty overhanging the top. Fill with the nectarine slices (keep the juices), add a little sugar to sweeten then cover with the overhanging filo pastry. Brush with melted butter and bake for 20-30mins. or until the pastry is crisp and brown. Slice to serve hot, warm or cold with the reserved juices, or with whipped cream into which the juices have been added.

Lazy Cook tips – *this pie is quite delicious. You will read from the instructions on the packet that filo pastry should be kept covered with a damp cloth until it is baked to prevent it becoming brittle and difficult to handle – I cover it with damp kitchen roll. Have all the filling ingredients prepared before assembling the pie. If the overlapping pastry does not completely cover the top, add more layers creased into folds to make an attractive topping. Buy fresh filo and any remaining can be frozen for future use. Always wash fresh fruit before eating.*

Poached Peaches with Amaretto Cream

to serve 4
4 peaches
sugar syrup (recipe below)
8 Amaretti biscuits
6 tbls. (approximately) Amaretto liqueur
300ml. (½pt) double cream
a handful of flaked almonds – browned

Set oven at gas 4/400°f/200°c/Aga baking oven.
Cut each peach in half and remove the stone. Place the peach halves, cut side up, in a shallow ovenproof dish, pour the hot sugar syrup over then cover and bake in the pre-set oven until the flesh has softened (this should take 20-30mins. depending on the ripeness of the peaches). Put the peaches (cut side up) into a serving dish and fit an Amaretti biscuit (flat side up) into the centre cavity. Pour a generous teaspoon of the liqueur on to each biscuit. Add 2 tbls. liqueur to the cream and whip to a soft peak, spoon it on to each peach and scatter with almonds. Serve warm.

Lazy Cook tips – the peaches can be left to bake while a main course is being eaten and the toppings added in a few minutes. The sugar syrup can be kept for future use – store in a covered jar in a refrigerator.

Sugar Syrup – dissolve 2 dessertspoons granulated sugar in 300ml (½pt) of boiling water. Flavour with a teaspoon orange flower water (optional).

Plum and Almond Pudding

to serve 6-8
50gms (2ozs) margarine
50gms (2ozs) flour
½ teas. baking powder
50gms (2ozs) caster sugar
25gms (1oz) ground almonds
1 large egg
8-10 drops almond essence
500gms (1 lb) plums – cut in half and remove stones
1 desst. demerara sugar for topping

Set oven at gas 4/400°f/200°c/Aga baking oven.
Oil a shallow cake tin (approx. 18cms./7" in diameter). Put the flour, caster sugar and almonds into a food processor and process for a few seconds. Add the margarine, egg and almond essence and process until smooth. Spread into the prepared tin and cover with the plum halves (cut side down). Scatter with demerara sugar and bake in the pre-set oven for 45mins. or until firm to the touch. Serve hot or warm with cream, ice-cream or custard. When cold serve as a cake.

Lazy Cook tips – bake this in a tin with a loose base if you have one. Stand the tin on a baking tray to bake in case the ingredients spill over. Choose Victoria plums if available. The texture is slightly soggy, the flavours are more-ish!

Rhubarb and Strawberry Crumble

serves 6-8
700-900gms (1½-2lbs) rhubarb
225gms (8ozs) fresh strawberries
225gms (8ozs) plain flour
100gms (4ozs) butter – cut into pieces
125gms (5ozs) demerara sugar

Set oven at gas 6/450°f/220°c/Aga roasting oven.

Top tail and wipe the rhubarb with damp kitchen paper before cutting into approximately 3cms (1") lengths. Put 2-3 tbls. cold water into a shallow ovenproof dish, add the prepared rhubarb and sprinkle with a tablespoon of the sugar. Slice or quarter the strawberries and place these over the rhubarb. Put the flour, half the remaining sugar and butter into a food processor and process for a few seconds to form a breadcrumb texture, spread over the strawberries and scatter the remaining sugar on top. Stand the dish on a baking tray and bake in the pre-set oven for approx. 30mins. or until the rhubarb has softened and the pudding is hot and bubbly. Serve straight from the oven with single cream or ice-cream or custard.

Lazy Cook tips – *just one of the advantages of crumbles is that they can be left to bake while a main course is being eaten. Test that the rhubarb has softened by piercing with a skewer – a delicious pudding to serve at the beginning of summer when new season's rhubarb is at its best. I prefer to make crumbles with butter, but this can be substituted for margarine – do not over-process, you will be left with pastry rather than a crumble mix. Stand the dish on a baking tray to cook in case any juices spill over.*

Stewed Rhubarb

Top, and tail and wipe the rhubarb with damp kitchen paper before cutting into approx. 3cms (1") lengths. Put into a pan with just a little water and a handful of fresh strawberries and simmer, with lid on pan, until the rhubarb softens. Sweeten to taste with clear honey or sugar. Serve hot, warm or cold with cream, ice cream or custard – 'simply' delicious!

Lazy Cook tips – *this is one of the few recipes I have from my late Mother, she called it "Strawberry Rhubarb". If you cook by Aga bring to a simmer on the slow hob then put into the simmering oven to continue cooking.*

<u>Sorbet</u> - this is another invaluable ingredient to have in store Traditionally sorbet is served between the main course and pudding to clear the palette. It can also be used as a base on which to pile fresh fruit and top with thick cream to make another very refreshing pudding to serve on a hot summer day.

Elderflower Sorbet

900mls (1½pts) water
350gms (12ozs) caster sugar
20 ripe elderflower heads – wash and dry
2 lemons – juice
1 egg white
sprigs of mint

Put the water and sugar into a pan and stir over a gentle heat until the sugar has dissolved.   Remove from heat and add the elderflower heads and leave to cool before stirring in the lemon juice.   Pour into a plastic container with lid and put into a freezer until it begins to set (30-45mins).   Whisk the egg white to a soft peak, take the mixture from the freezer and process for a few seconds then stir it into whisked whites.   Pack into the freezer container, cover and freeze.   To serve, scoop or spoon out into small glasses and decorate with a sprig of mint.

Lazy Cook tips – elder trees grow in most hedgerows and in many gardens, they produce clusters of small white-ish flowers at the beginning of summer which turn to dark berries in the autumn.   Pick them when the flowers are ripe (open and fresh in appearance) and preferably before the rain soaks them.   Wash before use.

Lemon Sorbet

4 lemons
225gms (8ozs) granulated sugar
600ml (1 pt) water
2 egg whites

Peel the zest from the lemons and put in a large pan with the sugar and water, stir continually until the sugar has dissolved. Bring to boiling point and boil rapidly for 6mins. Remove from heat and add the juice from the lemons and when cold put into a plastic or suitable container with a lid and freeze until it begins to set. Whisk the egg whites until stiff. Take the mixture from the freezer and process for a few seconds then stir it into the whisked whites. Pack into the freezer container, cover and freeze. To serve, scoop or spoon out into small glasses and top with a little grated lemon zest.

Fresh Strawberry Millefeuille

serves 6-8
350gms (12ozs) pkt ready rolled puff pastry
300ml (½pt) double cream
150ml (¼pt) single cream
500gms (1 lb) fresh strawberries – sliced
water icing (recipe below)

Set oven at gas 7/475°f/230°c/Aga roasting oven.
Cut the pastry into two pieces, place on a wet baking tray, prick all over with a fork and bake in the pre-set oven for 8-10mins. or until the pastry has risen and is brown on top. Turn the pastry over (using a fish slice), and bake for a further 5-10mins. or until cooked. Remove from oven and cool on a wire tray. To assemble, put one piece of cooked pastry on to a gateau plate (or a tray covered with foil). Whip the creams together to a soft peak and spread half over the pastry, top with the strawberry slices then spread with the remaining cream. Place the remaining pastry on top and spread with water icing. Slice to serve.

Lazy Cook tips – ready-rolled puff pastry can be purchased from a supermarket which makes this pudding accessible to "Lazy Cooks". Always keep some in a freezer and follow the directions on the packet for thawing and baking. A similar Millefeuille can be made with raspberries or any other soft fruit.

Water Icing - mix sieved icing sugar with a few spots of fresh lemon juice and cold water until the desired consistency.

Fresh Strawberry Shortbread with fresh Apricot Sauce

to serve 6
4 shortbread plates (recipe below)
425ml (¾pt) double cream
4 tbls. milk
500gms (1 lb) fresh strawberries
icing sugar
fresh apricot sauce - optional (recipe page 76)

Set aside 4 of the choicest strawberries (with husks).   Add the milk to the cream and whisk to a soft peak.   Assemble directly on to a gateau plate (or round tray covered with foil), by sandwiching the shortbread plates with the cream and the remaining strawberries, sliced.   Sieve the top with icing sugar and pile the reserved strawberries in the centre.   Slice to serve.

Lazy Cook tips *– assemble this pudding about an hour before it is to be served to allow the shortbread to soften a little making it easier to slice. It is delicious served with or without the apricot sauce.   This is another example of the kind of luxury presentation Lazy Cook's can achieve.*

Shortbread Plates

to make 4
100gms (4ozs) butter – softened
125gms (5 ozs) plain flour
25gms (1 oz) ground rice
50gms (2ozs) caster sugar

Set oven at gas 4/400°f/200°c/Aga baking oven.
Put the flour, rice and sugar into a processor and process for a few seconds to mix together.   Add the butter and process until it forms a ball, remove from processor and cut into 4 pieces.   Roll each piece between sheets of greaseproof paper into thin rounds approximately 20cms (8") in diameter. Place on baking sheets (in the paper) and bake for 6-8mins. or until they turn a light biscuit colour (in the paper).   Cool on a wire tray.

Lazy Cook tips – *you will find the paper will peel away from the baked sheets very easily. Handle with care but should they break you will be able to place them together when assembling the pudding - try to keep one undamaged for the top. They can be made in advance and will remain crisp for 3-4 weeks if stored in an airtight tin or polythene bags – store them in the greaseproof in which they were baked. A most useful ingredient to have in store.*

Fresh Apricot Sauce

500gms (1 lb) fresh apricots
150ml (¼pt) water
strips of rind from ½ a fresh lemon
juice of 1 orange
sugar to taste

Cut the apricots in half and remove the stones. Simmer the apricots with the lemon rind in the water, with lid on pan, until they soften (approx. 10mins). Remove the lemon rind, put the apricots into a food processor or liquidiser and process for a few seconds until smooth. Stir into the pan juices with the orange juice. Sweeten to taste and serve hot, warm or cold.

Lazy Cook tips – *this sauce can be made in advance and stored in a covered jar in a refrigerator until needed. Serve within 5 days.*

Summer Pudding

900gms (2lbs) mixed currants (black, red and white)
sugar or honey to taste
several slices of white bread – crusts removed

Wash the fruit and remove from the stalks. Put 50mls (2ozs) water into a pan, add the fruit, put lid on pan and simmer gently until the fruit has softened. Sweeten to taste and allow to cool. Line a basin with bread and fill to within 2cms/1" to the top with the cooked fruit removing it with a slotted spoon. Pour on enough of the juice from the pan to cover the fruit and top with more bread. To press, put a saucer on top with a 500gms (1 lb) weight on the saucer. Put into a cold larder or a refrigerator for

24hrs. before turning out on to a serving dish.   Pile whipped double cream on top and slice to serve.

Lazy Cook tips – like so many traditional puddings summer pudding has become very popular over the past few years.   There are numerous ways of making this truly delicious dessert, but the above is how I was taught to make it many years ago.   As the pudding rests the bread becomes soaked in the fruit juice.   Any additional juice should be kept to serve with the pudding or, should any bread not have soaked up the juices, pour on a little of the reserved juice before serving.

Trifles

Blackcurrant Trifle

serves 6-8
1 pkt trifle sponges
1 jar (680gms) blackcurrants in syrup
150ml (¼pt) double cream
25gms (1oz) bitter chocolate

Split the trifle sponges and put half of them into a trifle dish, cover with half the blackcurrants and some of the juice, top with the remaining trifle sponges, blackcurrants and juice.   Allow the juice to penetrate the sponges before spreading with lightly whipped cream and scattering with shavings of bitter chocolate.

Lazy Cook tips – this recipe will be familiar to those who have my 'Lazy Cook's Christmas' or who listen to my radio broadcasts.   However, it is far too popular a recipe for me not to print it again, not least because it is made in minutes. but also because it is so delicious.   In summer I serve this trifle with a small collection of summer flowers and herbs in the centre – nasturtium flowers, perfumed geraniums (flowers and leaf), small sprigs of mint and strands of chive. 'Lazy Cook's' do not have time to pick blackcurrants, or to cook fresh ones; the jars I recommend are excellent in flavour and no 'Lazy Cook' should be without at least one jar in store.

'Traditional' Trifle made with Peaches and Brandy

to serve 6-8
600ml. (1pt) full cream milk
2 desst. custard powder
1 teas. vanilla essence
1 desst. granulated sugar
1 pkt. trifle sponges
peach jam
150ml. (¼pt) brandy
4-6 peaches – stone and slice
300ml. (½pt) double or whipping cream
flaked almonds – browned
glacé cherries

Mix the custard powder to a smooth paste with a little of the milk. Warm the remaining milk, add the custard powder paste, vanilla essence and sugar and stir until it boils and thickens, remove from heat. Split the trifle sponges and spread with jam before putting into a trifle dish. Cover with a generous amount of brandy and mash a little with a fork. Cover with the peach slices then the made custard and leave to become cold. To serve, cover with lightly whipped cream, scatter with almonds and dot with glacé cherries

Lazy Cook tips – the custard should not be of too thick a consistency when boiled, if it is it will be solid when cold and spoil the texture of the trifle. For trifles made with baked egg custard see next page. Make a day in advance and store, covered, in a refrigerator or cold larder. Add whipped cream, nuts and cherries to serve.

Upsidedown Peach Trifle

to serve 6
1 baked egg custard - cold (recipe below)
125gms (4ozs) Amaretti biscuits
6 tbls. (approx) Amaretto liqueur
1 tbls. orange marmalade
150ml. (¼pt) double or whipping cream
4 peaches – stone and slice

Soak the biscuits in liqueur and as they soften mash them with a fork. Spread marmalade over the cold baked custard, then the soaked biscuits. Cover with whipped cream and top with peach slices arranged slightly overlapping.

Lazy Cook tips *– bake the custard a few days in advance in readiness to make the trifle. Store, covered, in a refrigerator.   A similar trifle can be made with strawberries or raspberries (recipe page 80).*

Baked Egg Custard

425ml. (¾pt) full cream milk
1 desst. granulated sugar
1 teas. vanilla essence
3 large eggs – whisked together
25gms. (1oz) butter - optional
freshly grated nutmeg.

Warm the milk and sugar in a pan before pouring it on to the whisked eggs. Stir in the vanilla essence and pour it, through a sieve, into an 850ml. (1½pt) porcelain soufflé dish. Add the butter and freshly grated nutmeg. Cover with a double thickness of buttered greaseproof and tie with string. Stand the dish in a pan and add warm water (bain marie), to come approximately half way up the dish. Bake in the pre-set oven for 10mins. before reducing the temperature to gas 3/300°f/150°c/Aga simmering oven, until the custard has set. Remove from the oven, lift out of the baking pan and leave to become cold. Serve, or store in a refrigerator until needed, use within 4 days.

Lazy Cook tips - baked custard is delicious served with or without accompaniments. The butter will give it a creamy crust.

Upsidedown Strawberry Trifle

to serve 6
1 baked egg custard - cold (recipe page 79)
1 pkt sponge fingers
150ml (¼pt) sweet sherry
150ml (¼pt) double or whipping cream
500gms (1 lb) strawberries

Soak the sponge fingers in a generous amount of sherry and as they soften mash them with a fork. Cover the top of the cold custard with some of the strawberries, sliced. Top with the sponge finger mixture and finally spread with the cream whipped to a soft peak. Cover completely with whole strawberries (some with husks).

Lazy Cook tips – bake the custard a few days in advance and store, covered, in a refrigerator, the toppings can then be added in a few minutes. Sponge Fingers are sometimes sold as Boudoir Biscuits. A similar trifle can be made with whole raspberries or peaches - see Upsidedown Peach Trifle (recipe page 79).

SALADS

There are of course umpteen ways of serving a lettuce leaf and other salad ingredients, but my advice as a Lazy Cook, is 'keep it simple'. They all take time to wash, cut up and prepare, much of which, because of the nature of the ingredient, needs to be done at the last minute. Always remember, too many choices are unnecessary and they confuse the palette.

Beetroot Salad

beetroots – cooked (recipe page 103)
fresh French tarragon leaves
vinaigrette (basic recipe on page page 82)

Peel and slice the beetroots into a serving dish. Cover with vinaigrette and scatter with tarragon leaves. Leave to marinate before serving.

Lazy Cook tips – if the beetroots are small they can be served whole. The flavours complement each other well.

Mixed Green Salad

lettuce – different varieties
lambs lettuce
land cress
wild strawberries - optional
vinaigrette (recipe page 82)

Wash and dry all the salad ingredients, mix into a salad bowl and toss in vinaigrette just before serving.

Lazy Cook tips – a Salad Spinner is perfect for drying lettuce. Wash and dry a quantity and store in a polythene bag in a refrigerator ready for daily use.

Vinaigrette

Basic Recipe
2/3rd sunflower and extra virgin olive oil mixed
1/3rd vinegar – wine, cider or herb
freshly ground pepper

Put all the ingredients into a jar and shake before serving

Lazy Cook tips - *make a quantity in readiness for daily use. The flavour and texture can be changed by adding mustards, chopped fresh herbs or chopped onion. Experiment with different flavours to suit your palette.*

New Potato Salad (1)

new potatoes
oil
chives – cut up
freshly grated nutmeg

Prepare the potatoes by scrubbing or peeling and cut into mouth-sized pieces then boil until they are firm but edible. Strain the liquid from the pan, add the remaining ingredients and stir. Pile into a dish and serve warm, or cold.

New Potato Salad (2)

new potatoes
freshly grated nutmeg
mayonnaise (recipe page 26)
chopped parsley

Prepare the potatoes by scrubbing or peeling and cut into mouth-sized pieces then boil until they are firm but edible. Strain the liquid from the pan and allow the potatoes to become cold before seasoning with grated nutmeg and coating with mayonnaise and freshly chopped parsley. Pile into a dish to serve.

Mixed Tomato Salad

to serve 8-10 portions
6 tomatoes – cut into 4 or 6 pieces
1 cucumber – cut into cubes (without skin)
1 red, or salad onion – skin and chop
250gms (½lb) pitted black olives
250gms (½lb) seedless grapes
1 bunch radishes – cut in half or quarters
1 tbls. mixed fresh herbs – chopped
vinaigrette – basic recipe

Mix all together in a bowl several hours before serving, stir occasionally.

Lazy Cook tips – this is an excellent salad to serve, the colours and flavours are good. It is an excellent salad to make if catering for a crowd as it improves as it marinates, it also avoids having lots of dishes of different ingredients. Prepare in advance and store in a polythene bag in a refrigerator. This is a very popular salad and I am constantly being asked how it is made.

Tomato and Fresh Basil

Tomatoes - sliced
fresh basil leaves
vinaigrette – basic recipe

Layer the tomato slices with fresh basil leaves and cover with vinaigrette - leave to marinate before serving.

SAUCES/FILLINGS/PASTES

Savoury Sauces

Bechamel (recipe page 121)
Burnt Pepper Sauce (recipe page 44)
Cream Pepper Sauce (recipe page 27)
Mayonnaise (basic recipe 26)
Mayonnaise - orange (recipe page 121)
Mediterranean Sauce (recipe page 36)
Mediterranean Cream Sauce (recipe page 51)
Parsley Sauce (recipe page 37)
Quick Tomato Sauce (recipe page 41)
Spicy Cream Sauce (recipe page 29)
Sweet Basil Dressing (recipe page 119)
Vinaigrette (recipe page 82)

Sweet Sauces

Caramel Sauce (recipe page 63)
Fresh Apricot Sauce (recipe page 76)
Fresh Plum Sauce (recipe page 15)

Savoury/Fillings/Pastes

Parsley and Thyme Stuffing (recipe page 47)
Savoury Filling (1) - (recipe page 118)
Savoury Filling (2) - (recipe page 118)
Savoury Paste (recipe page 18)
Vegetable Farce (recipe page 110)

SOUPS and STOCKS

<u>Courgette and Orange Soup</u>

to serve 4-6
1 medium onion – skin and chop
500gms (1 lb) courgettes – wash, top and tail and slice
6 fresh sage leaves (or several good pinches dried)
600ml (1 pt) chicken or vegetable stock
300ml (½pt) orange juice (from a carton)
garnish –
150ml. (¼pt single cream) – optional
grated zest of 1 fresh orange

Soften the onion in a little boiling water with lid on pan. Add the prepared courgettes and the sage and simmer, with lid on pan, for 3-4 mins. to soften the courgettes. Purée in a food processor or liquidiser then return to the pan. Add the stock and orange juice and stir before simmering for 10mins. with lid on pan. Pour into a jug and when cold, cover and put into a refrigerator. Serve from the refrigerator with a swirl of cream and grated orange zest on each portion.

Lazy Cook tips – *I prefer this soup served cold, it will provide a refreshing start to a meal on a hot day. Use within 4 days*

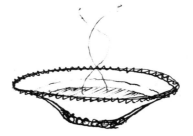

Courgette and Tomato Soup

to serve 4
3 courgettes – wash, top and tail and slice
2 cloves garlic – skin and chop
1 x 230gm. tin chopped tomatoes
1 tbls. fresh chopped herbs to include oregano and basil
8 spring onions – slice thickly
¼ teas. celery salt
1 teas. Worcestershire sauce
600ml (1pt) vegetable or chicken stock
garnish (optional)
single cream
fresh basil leaves

Add the courgettes, onions and garlic to a pan containing a little boiling water and boil, with lid on pan, for 2-3mins. or until the courgettes have begun to soften. Put the solid ingredients into a processor or liquidiser with the tomatoes and process to a purée. Return to the pan and add all the remaining ingredients, bring to a simmer and simmer gently, with lid on pan for 15-20mins. Pour into a jug and when cold, cover and put into a refrigerator. Serve from the refrigerator with a swirl of cream and a basil leaf on each portion. This soup can also be served hot straight from the pan.

Lazy Cook tips – cold soups provide a most refreshing start to a meal on a hot day. This is a quick soup to make with a good blend of summer flavours which develop on the palette.

Melon and Ginger Soup

to serve 4-6
1 medium onion – skin and chop
1 large melon
600ml (1 pt) chicken or vegetable stock
1-2 teas. fresh ginger – grated
150ml. (¼pt) double cream

Soften the onion in a little boiling water with lid on pan. Cut the melon in half and discard the seeds. Spoon out the flesh and process or liquidise, with the softened onion and ginger to purée Stir the processed ingredients into the stock and when cold store, covered, for several hours in a refrigerator. Stir in the cream before serving.

Lazy Cook tips – make this soup with a pink fleshed melon. Make it the day before it is needed. Use within 4 days.

Pea and Ham Soup

serves 4-6
1 large onion – skin and chop
1 x 200gm pkt lardons (chopped bacon)
900ml (1½pts) chicken stock
2 tbls. plain flour
little milk
1 x 200gm. tin petits pois
fresh mint (or dried)
75ml. (2ozs) single cream

Smear the base of a large pan with oil and when hot add the prepared onion and lardons, stir and cook over a gently heat, with lid on pan. Add the flour to a little cold milk and mix to a smooth, runny paste. Add the stock, and the flour mixture to the pan and stir continuously over a gentle heat until it boils and boil for about a minute. Add the petits pois and a good handful of fresh chopped mint (or 1 teas. dried), bring to a simmer, place lid on pan and simmer for 5-10mins. Allow to become cold before storing overnight, covered, in a refrigerator.   To serve (straight from the refrigerator), stir in the cream and ladle into individual soup bowls.

Lazy Cook tips – this soup can also be served hot. Use within 4 days. I use a mixture of chicken and ham stock in this recipe. The thickening with flour is optional. This is a quick soup to make and good served cold or hot, make it with fresh garden mint, if available.

Summary Vegetable Soup

to serve 6-8
1 red onion – skin and slice into rings
selection of summer vegetables to include –
young carrots – scrub and slice into rings
asparagus stalks
broad beans
French beans – cut in half
courgettes – cut into slices or sticks
good squeeze fresh lemon juice
freshly ground white pepper
1 lt. (2pts) stock – chicken or vegetable
1 tbls. mixed fresh herbs - chopped
a good handful chopped watercress
garnish -
chives
cream – optional

Put the prepared vegetables into a pan containing a little boiling water and boil for a few minutes with lid on pan.   Add the remaining ingredients, except the garnish, bring to a simmer and simmer with lid on pan for 20-30mins.   Add the watercress and simmer for a further 5mins. with lid on pan.   Pour into a jug and when cold, cover and put into a refrigerator. Serve from the refrigerator with a swirl of cream and chopped chives on each portion.   This soup can also be served hot straight from the pan.

Lazy Cook tips – include small quantities of each vegetable. The herbs I recommend for this soup are sage, thyme, parsley and lemon balm.   I use a mixture of chicken and ham stock (home-made stock recipes on page 89). Bought stock can be used.   Adjust the amount of stock according to the amount of vegetables.   Store when cold, covered, in a cold larder or refrigerator, use within 3 days.   A delicious soup, full of all the colours and flavours of summer.   Liquidise or process the solid ingredients if you prefer.   Cold soups provide a most refreshing start to a meal on a hot day.

STOCKS

Stock Making the Lazy Cook way

There is something very wholesome and satisfying about adding a little jellied stock to a recipe. My method of making stock, though not traditional, gives good quick results and a stock superior to any which can be bought.

Fish – put uncooked fish bones, skin and heads into a pan and cover with cold water. Bring slowly to boil, without lid, skim the top then add 8-10 peppercorns and a bay leaf. Place lid on pan and simmer for 20mins. Remove from heat and strain into a basin. Follow instructions for storing or freezing as for meat stock.

Ham – strain the liquid from a cooked ham or bacon joint, (recipe page 35). Follow directions for storing as for meat stock.

Meat – put bones/carcass, cook or uncooked into a pan. Cover with cold water, bring slowly to boil, without lid. Skim the top, place lid on pan and simmer for 2-4 hrs (if you cook by Aga this should be done in the simmering oven). Strain into a basin and when cold store in a fridge and use within 2 days, removing the fat which will have set on the surface. Alternatively freeze by removing the surface fat and pack the stock into freezer bags. For convenience of use I freeze stock in bags of varying sizes.

Vegetable – strain all liquid from cooked vegetables into a jug and when cold cover and store in a fridge. Use within 2 days.

STARTERS and LIGHT MEALS

Cherry Tomatoes with a Savoury Filling (recipe page 118).

Chicken Liver Parcels

makes approx. 16
250gms (8ozs) chicken livers
4 ox tongue slices, not too thinly sliced – cut each into 4 strips
coarse grain mustard
16 rashers rindless streaky bacon

Set oven at gas 6/450°f/220°c/Aga roasting oven.
Roll each liver in a strip of tongue.   Stretch each rasher with a knife then spread with mustard and roll it round the ox tongue.   Thread several on to a metal skewer (or individual cocktail sticks), put on to a shallow baking tin (or a swiss roll tin) and bake in the pre-set oven for 10-15mins. or until the bacon has cooked – turn half-way through baking.   Serve hot or cold.

Lazy Cook tips – this is a very versatile recipe, quick to prepare and bake, colourful and full of good flavours. I serve them hot or cold.   As a starter I serve them on a little salad drizzled with vinaigrette.   I also serve them with a platter of cold meats, whole or sliced.   Make them smaller and serve as canapés.   Make in advance and store, in a parcel, in a refrigerator – an invaluable ingredient to have in store, especially good for impromptu entertaining – very 'Lazy Cook'.

Courgettes with Savoury Fillings (recipe page 107).

Egg Mayonnaise with Anchovy and (Wild) Strawberries

large eggs – boiled for 6-7mins
mayonnaise – home-made if possible (recipe page 26)
anchovy fillets – 2 per egg
a few wild (or small) strawberries
chives – cut into strips approx. 4cms (1½")

Shell eggs and cut in half lengthways, put in the centre of a serving dish or individual plates – cut side down.   Coat each half with mayonnaise, place a curl of anchovy on top and 'spike' with chives.   Pile a few strawberries alongside.   Serve with brown bread and butter.

Lazy Cook tips – I think the eggs for this recipe are nicer if they are boiled for a short time and the centre yolk is slightly soft.   I recommend anchovy fillets preserved in oil and available from delicatessen and supermarkets by weight.   About a dessertspoon of mayonnaise will be enough to coat each egg half.

Eggs in Savoury Jelly

600ml (1 pt) savoury jelly (recipe page 23)
6 cocktail gherkins
6 raddish – cut into thin slices, or strips
chives
6 small eggs – boil for 3-4mins.
garnish –
lambs lettuce
mayonnaise (recipe page 26)

Pour a little savoury jelly into 6 ramekin (or similar) dishes.   Cut the gherkins partway down so that they can be opened into a fan shape and put in the jelly with slices or strips of raddish and some chive strands to make a pattern.   Put into the refrigerator to set before placing an egg in each dish and covering with liquid jelly – put back into the refrigerator to set.   To serve, dip each ramekin in hot water for a few seconds to loosen the jelly and turn on to a serving plate.   Garnish with lambs lettuce and serve with mayonnaise and brown bread and butter.

Lazy cook tips – *if serving these to vegetarians make the jelly using Gelezone (vegetarian gelatine) – follow the manufacturers directions to make up.   The decoration set into the jelly can be made from various ingredients, they make the eggs look very pretty when turned out.   Make in advance and store in a refrigerator, covered with clingfilm, use within 3 days.   Serve as suggested in the recipe or to decorate a large platter of fish or meat*

Fresh Herb and (wild) Strawberry Loaf

to cut 5-6 thick slices
100gms (4ozs) plain flour
1 teas. baking powder
few pinches ground white pepper
2 eggs
1 tbls. runny honey
2 ozs oil
1 tbls. Balsamic vinegar
1 desst. fresh lemon juice
2 handfuls fresh herbs (a selection of rosemary, coriander, basil, parsley, marjoram, thyme, sage)
a few fresh strawberries (wild if possible)

Set oven at gas 4/400°f/200°c/Aga baking oven.   Line the base of a 15cm (6") round tin with greaseproof and lightly oil.   Put the flour, baking powder and pepper into a food processor and process for a few seconds. Add all remaining ingredients, except the strawberries, and process for a few seconds until smooth.   Pour into the prepared tin, dot the top with wild (or small) strawberries and bake in the pre-set oven for 20-30mins. or until set.   Cool on a wire tray.   Slice to serve (see serving suggestion below and Lazy Cook tips).   Store in a polythene bag in a refrigerator. Use within 3 days.

Serving suggestion – my favourite way of serving this is to spread thick slices with butter which has been flavoured with sundried tomato purée.   Top this with a cornet of ox tongue (with a small filling of mixed green salad), and hold together with a large whole strawberry spiked on to a cocktail stick. Garnish with a pickled gherkin cut into a fan shape.

Lazy Cook tips – any oil can be used, or a mixture (include a little from a jar of sundried tomatoes, if you have some).   Choose a selection of your favourite herbs, preferably picked straight from the garden or a windowsill pot – these need not be chopped, cut them roughly, the processor will do the rest.   I recommend whole wild strawberries otherwise small fresh strawberries, cut in half, and placed cut side down.   This is a lovely bread to serve with salads, cold meats and many other summer ingredients.   The flavour is excellent and the texture smooth and light.

Mini Kebabs

roasted peppers, smoked salmon, grapes
nectarine or peach slices, salami, cherry tomatoes
parma ham, apricot halves, radish
Extra virgin olive oil mixed with a little balsamic vinegar

Thread these on to cocktail sticks.   Serve 3 to each person on a bed of mixed salad leaves and drizzle with the oil and vinegar dressing.

Lazy Cook tips – mix and match ingredients to suit your palette, or from ingredients you have in stock.   These provide colourful and refreshing starters.

Onion Flan

to serve 6
1 cooked pastry case
1 large onion – skin and slice into rings
10-12 fresh sage leaves (or 1 teas. dried)
50gms (2ozs) stilton cheese – grated
2 large eggs – whisk together
200ml. (8ozs) full cream milk
freshly ground white pepper

Set oven at gas 4/400°f/200°c/Aga baking oven.
Stand the pastry case on a baking tray.   Soften the onion rings in a little boiling water with lid on pan then, using a slotted spoon, put them to cover the base of the pastry case and top with the sage leaves and stilton.   Warm the milk and add to the whisked eggs, whisk together before pouring, through a sieve, on to the pastry case ingredients.   Season with pepper and bake in the pre-set oven for 20-30mins. or until set and browning on top. Serve warm or cold, cut into slices.

Lazy Cook tips – for a richer flavour a mixture of single cream and full cream milk can be used.   As the flan sets it will also rise.   A tasty flan to serve.

Pastry Bases topped with Savoury Butter, Black Pudding and Tomato
(recipe page 10)

Pastry Bases topped with Savoury Butter, Ox Tongue and Cornichons
(recipe page 10)

Pastry Bases topped with Herb Cheese and Fresh Strawberries
(recipe page 10)

Pitta Parcels with Mushrooms and Baby Sweetcorn perfumed with Fennel Fern

to make 4
4 pitta breads
225gms (8ozs) button mushrooms (wipe with damp kitchen roll)
1 pkt baby sweetcorn (cut each in half)
a dash of mushroom ketchup
freshly ground pepper
a few pinches strong curry powder
2-3tbls single cream
fresh fennel fern

Cook the pitta breads following the manufacturers instructions and open at the top or side – keep warm.   Soften the mushrooms and baby corn in a little water with lid on pan, stir in the remaining ingredients before packing into the pitta parcels or put the filling into a bowl and allow everyone to help themselves.

Pitta Parcels with Summer Salad and a Herb Vinaigrette

pitta bread
mixed lettuce leaves – wash and dry
handful of wild strawberries - optional
tomatoes – cut up
cucumber – cut into cubes (without skin)
red, or salad onion – skin and chop
pitted black olives
seedless grapes
radishes – cut in half or quarters
anchovies preserved in oil
mixed fresh herbs – chopped
vinaigrette (recipe page 82)

Cook the pitta breads following the manufacturers instructions and open at the top or side.   Mix all the above ingredients together and pack into the pitta bread. If there is time allow the mixed salad to marinate in the vinaigrette.

Prawn and Melon Platter - (recipe page 21)

Fresh Salmon Bake – (recipe page 26)

Sandwiches

Sandwiches must be amongst the most 'convenient' of 'convenience foods'. They can be eaten while sitting, standing, talking, walking, hot or cold, in or out of doors. Furthermore, the minimum of equipment is needed to prepare them – what other meal could be more versatile? At their best they are delicious, prepared badly they are boring. I like the fillings of sandwiches to be tasty, well seasoned and plentiful – all ingredients hanging out and with no empty corners. When I was a child sandwiches were served for tea at weekends and my late Father's favourite fillings were salmon, made from tinned salmon mashed to a paste with vinegar and salt and pepper – I can taste them now. Amongst my favourites, especially in summer, are watercress seasoned with plenty of salt; cucumber, lettuce, soggy tomato, cream cheese and parsley, fish paste, and jam. For a 'platter of sandwiches' I recommend the bread is spread with a little cream cheese instead of butter (or your choice of spread), before being sandwiched together with a slice of ham.

Platter of Sandwiches

allow 1 sandwich per person made from 2 rounds of bread
savoury fillings – of your choice
mayonnaise or mustard
garnish -
tomatoes – cut into quarters
hard boiled eggs – shell and cut into quarters
radishes – cut into halves
salad cress

Cut the made sandwiches into quarters and arrange, slightly overlapping, on a large serving dish. Garnish with the prepared tomatoes, hard boiled eggs, and radishes, and scatter with salad cress.

Savoury Cheesecake Slices

to serve 8 slices
100gms (4ozs) plain flour
1 teas. baking powder
1 teas. caster sugar
3 large eggs
100gms (4ozs) full fat cream cheese
good pinch ground white pepper
good pinch mustard powder
6 sundried tomatoes preserved in oil
garnish -
225gms (8 ozs) cream or curd cheese
a little milk
1 tbls. freshly chopped parsley
fresh chives
radishes
spring onions – cut into short lengths
rocket or basil leaves

Set oven at gas 4/400°f/200°c/Aga baking oven.
Line the base of a 17cm (7") round cake tin with greaseproof paper and oil all over. Put all the ingredients (except the garnish) into a food processor and process until smooth. Pour into the prepared tin and bake in the pre-set oven for 25-30mins. or until set. Cool on a wire tray. To garnish, cut the cake into 8 slices. Soften the cheese with a little milk and work in the chopped parsley, spread this thickly on to each slice then top with a collection of the garnish ingredients arranged in a cluster. To serve, re-shape the individual slices into a cake on one large serving dish, or serve on individual plates. Serve as a starter or a light meal with salad.

Lazy Cook tips - I recommend cake tin liners made from baking parchment when making this and similar cakes – they need no oiling and keep all the ingredients contained during baking. To serve as a starter slice into smaller pieces. This cake can be made and stored in an airtight polythene bag in a refrigerator. Bring back to room temperature to serve and use within 4 days. A colourful cake with a good savoury flavour and much enjoyed by vegetarians.

Spinach with Bacon and Tomato Concertinas

to serve 4
4 thick rashers bacon – without rind
4 tomatoes
oil
4 slices of toast
butter or margarine - optional
500gms (1 lb) spinach purée (recipe page 115)

Set oven at gas 6/450°f/220°c/Aga roasting oven.   Gather each bacon slice together, tuck a tomato slice between each fold and secure with a cocktail stick.   Place on a baking or swiss roll tin, brush with oil and bake until the bacon is cooked.   Spread the toast with butter then with spinach purée and top with a bacon and tomato concertina, remove the cocktail sticks   Serve hot or cold.

Lazy Cook tips – these can be baked in the oven or under a hot grill.

Soups *(recipes on pages 85-88)*

VEGETABLES

As each summer approaches and I dig over the small vegetable patch in readiness for setting the early potatoes, I often think back to our early years in Bisley and in particular to my first introduction to the Bisley Flower Show when I was invited to join the committee. The Committee at that time was made up of a handful of excellent gardeners whose families had lived in the village for generations. They had learnt their gardening skills from their fathers and their grandfathers; they knew how to achieve the best results from the Bisley soil. Then there were a number of ladies who, as well as gardening, were talented flower arrangers, and myself.

The first meeting of the year was usually around Easter, and this was called to approve the new schedule in readiness for printing. As the many different classes were re-examined and the previous years entries picked over, the most fascinating discussions took place on the problems facing enthusiastic gardeners keen to exhibit the very best of their produce. "it was too wet for my leeks" says one. "The mice ate all my peas" comments another. "The sun came just in time to ripen my tomatoes" says another, and so on. My gardening skills at that time were somewhat limited and I had little to contribute to this conversation, but as I listened to these professionals who made it all sound so easy, I would feel myself getting completely carried away by the temptations a packet of seeds offered. I would leave the meeting confident that next year I would be able to join in this garden talk - tomorrow I will dig up the lawn and start to garden in earnest, I would tell myself, but it takes me no longer than the short walk home to realise how impractical this would be and in any case I'm going out tomorrow!

Here my reverie ends, but my excitement and anticipation of the first taste of the new season's vegetables continues and inevitably my thoughts turn to new ways of presenting them. Some of these I share with you in the following recipes – I do hope you will enjoy them.

Most vegetables need to be par-boiled, boiled, steamed or cooked in some way before they can be served. Unless otherwise stated, I cook vegetables in a pan in the smallest amount of water – often by the time the vegetables have softened, the water has evaporated. I recommend all water strained from cooked vegetables (now vegetable stock), is kept and used to flavour soups and sauces. It should be kept in a covered container in a refrigerator and used within 3 days. I do not add salt when cooking vegetables.

Asparagus

Regretfully, I think, because so many vegetables are available all year round much of the luxury has been taken from them, but for me there is nothing to compare with the flavour of the first Evesham asparagus. It doesn't need dressing up, just simply cooked and served. Serve it as a starter with thin bread and butter or as a vegetable course with fresh salmon.

To cook asparagus

Snap the white-ish, tough end from the top and discard. Wash the remaining green stalks and lay them in a pan containing a little boiling water. Place lid on pan and cook for 2-3mins. or until the asparagus is tender. Strain off the cooking liquid and keep. To serve, put the asparagus on to a hot serving dish, or individual plates, and smear with butter.

Lazy Cook tips – *take care not to damage the delicate seedpod like tips by using kitchen tongs when removing the cooked asparagus from the pan. I recommend asparagus is not cooked for too long, it needs to retain its delicate flavour which is enhanced with butter. Spike a lump of butter on to a knife and wipe this over the hot asparagus, place the remainder on top and it will melt into the asparagus. Serve immediately it is cooked. Use the cooking liquid to flavour sauces or when cooking other vegetables, store, covered, in a refrigerator.*

Aubergine - when I refer back to my original evening class notes, I read the comment at the end of the first aubergine recipe I cooked – 'not bad'! But over the years I have persevered and in doing so have discovered the versatility of this vegetable (sometimes known as an Egg Plant). It has good nutritious values; rich in protein it is a popular vegetarian alternative to meat and other high protein foods. The following are just a few recipes resulting from my experiments.

Baked Aubergine with Mushrooms and Fresh Thyme

to serve 2
1 medium/large aubergine
a little oil
1 medium onion – skin and chop
125gms (4ozs) mushrooms – chop
1 teas. mushroom ketchup
a little vegetable stock or hot water
2 sundried tomatoes preserved in oil – cut into strips
several good pinches fresh thyme leaves
freshly ground white pepper
50gms (2ozs) cashew nuts – browned and coarsely chopped
2 tbls. jumbo oats
50gms (2ozs) parmesan cheese - shavings

Set oven at gas 6/220°f/220°c/Aga roasting oven.
Wash and top and tail the aubergine then cut in half lengthways. Remove the flesh and keep. Mark the flesh side of the aubergine with crosses and brush with oil, brush the skin with oil and place, skin side up, in an ovenproof dish which has been moistened with a film of cold water. Bake in the pre-set oven for 10-15mins. to soften. Meanwhile, add the prepared onion to a pan containing a little boiling water, place lid on pan and cook until the onion begins to soften. Cut the aubergine flesh into small cubes and add to the onion with a little vegetable stock or water to prevent sticking and cook for 2-3mins. or until the aubergine begins to soften, with lid on pan.

Add the prepared mushrooms, mushroom ketchup, sundried tomatoes and thyme leaves, season with freshly ground white pepper and stir well. Remove the aubergine cases from the oven and pack with the prepared filling. Mix the prepared nuts with the oats and parmesan shavings and pile on to the aubergine. Return to oven and bake, uncovered, for 10-15mins. or until the topping is crisp and brown. Serve hot or cold.

Lazy Cook tips – I find a grapefruit knife will easily remove the aubergine flesh. If the aubergine skin is not softened before the filling is added, it will take for ever to cook and will considerably lengthen the cooking process

Aubergine Slices with Parmesan Cheese

to make 10-12
2 aubergines
oil
fresh thyme
2-3 large tomatoes
a sprinkling of granulated sugar
fresh basil leaves
freshly ground white pepper
175gms (6ozs) parmesan cheese - sliced

Wash and top and tail the aubergine before cutting into slices approximately 2cm. (½") thick. Heat 1 tbls. of oil in a large sauté or frying pan, brush both sides of each aubergine slice with oil, add to the pan and cook, over a low heat, until they soften (this will take 10-15mins). Remove from heat and top each slice with a little thyme then a slice of tomato with a sprinkling of sugar added. Season with freshly ground pepper before topping with a basil leaf and a slice of parmesan. Put under a hot grill until the cheese has melted. Serve as a starter with a little salad garnish, or a main course on a bed of Sweetcorn Rice (recipe page 102). The prepared slices are also excellent heated on a barbecue.

Lazy Cook tips – if you cook by Aga put the prepared slices into the top of the roasting oven until the cheese has melted. This recipe is full of flavour and colour, it is one of my favourite ways of serving aubergine. Avoid adding more oil during the initial cooking, cooked over a 'gentle' heat they should soften and not burn. Once assembled they can be stored, covered, in a refrigerator or cold larder in readiness to heat and serve in the oven or on a barbecue. Served on Sweetcorn Rice this is a very colourful and unusual meal and the combined flavours are good.

Aubergine Slices with Sweetcorn Rice

to serve 4
8-10 cooked aubergine slices with parmesan (recipe above)
250gms (8ozs) cooked rice (recipe page 53)
1 x 400gm tin sweetcorn in water
1 pickled cucumber – sliced
1 tbls. fresh parsley – chopped

To serve hot - put the sweetcorn and water into a large saucepan and bring to a simmer, add the cooked rice and cucumbers and stir over a gentle heat until they are hot. Strain off any liquid and stir in the parsley. Spread over the base of a large hot serving dish and put the cooked aubergine slices on top.

Lazy Cook tips – an excellent vegetarian recipe.

Beetroots – to cook

Cut off the leafy tops to approximately 2cms (1") from the beetroot then place the beetroots in a large pan, cover with water, bring to a simmer and simmer, with lid on pan, for approximately 1 hour. Strain off and discard the liquid and allow the beetroots to cool before storing in a refrigerator or cold larder, until required. Use within 4 days.

Lazy Cook tips – the length of the simmering process depends on the size and the age of the beetroots. If you cook by Aga the simmering process should be done in the simmering oven. The leafy tops, if not old or damaged, can be washed, and cooked as spinach (recipe page 115).

Roasted Beetroots

10-12 small new season's beetroots
oil
freshly ground black pepper

Set oven at gas 6/450°f/220°c/Aga roasting oven.
Wash and dry the beetroots well and trim off the tops to within 1cm (¼") of the beetroot. Heat 2 tbls. oil in a roasting tin or shallow ovenproof dish, add the prepared beetroots and coat each in the hot oil then season with freshly ground pepper. Put into the pre-set oven and roast for 45mins – 1 hr. or until the beetroots are tender. Serve hot.

Lazy Cook tips – new seasons beetroots can be purchased at most good farm shops or farmers' markets. The edible skin becomes crisp as they roast.

Whole Beetroots with Fresh Tarragon

to prepare 6-8 beetroots
small beetroots – cooked (recipe page 103)
4tbls. oil
3tbls. tarragon vinegar
½ teas. dried tarragon
freshly ground white pepper

Peel the cooked beetroots and pile into a serving dish.   Mix the oil, vinegar, tarragon and pepper together with a fork and pour on to the beetroots.   Leave to marinate before serving, stirring occasionally.

Lazy Cook tips – these are delicious served with summer salads. Small beetroots are available from most good farm shops or farmers' markets from the beginning of summer – it is a short season, serve them while it lasts.

Broad Beans - I prefer to buy these when they are young when they can be topped and tailed, cut into short lengths and cooked in the skins. Scatter them with fresh sage to serve.   Cooked this way they have a very different flavour.   As the pods develop I buy them and cook the beans only.

Whole Baby Carrots with Pumpkin Seeds

1 bunch new carrots with tops
25gms (1oz) butter
1 tbls. pumpkin seeds

Remove the tops and wash the carrots before boiling in a small amount of water, with lid on pan, until the water has evaporated and the carrots have begun to soften.   Add the butter to the pan and toss the carrots in this as it melts.   Stir in the pumpkin seeds before putting into a hot serving dish.

Lazy Cook tips – watch the carrots as the water evaporates so that they do not burn.   A colourful way of serving new baby carrots – they sometimes vary in size, cut any larger ones in half before cooking.

Baked Chicory

to serve 4
4 chicory heads
175gms (6ozs) white mushrooms – wipe and slice
a few spots mushroom ketchup
freshly ground white pepper
5fl.oz (¼pt) single cream

Set oven at gas 6/450°f/220°c/Aga roasting oven.
Cover the base of a shallow ovenproof dish with the prepared mushrooms
and season with a few spots mushroom ketchup.   Trim 1cm (½") stalk
from the base of each chicory and discard.   Slice the chicory lengthways
into 2 or 3 pieces and add to a pan containing about 5fl.oz (¼pt) of boiling
water, put lid on pan and simmer for a minute or two – remove from liquid
using kitchen tongs and place over the mushrooms, season lightly with
freshly ground pepper.   Boil the pan liquid until it reduces to
approximately 2tbls.   Stir in the cream and bring to a simmer before
pouring over the chicory.   Cover with foil and bake in the pre-set oven for
10-15mins. or until hot and bubbling.

*Lazy Cook tips – this can be heated in a hot oven as in the recipe, or under
a hot grill or in a microwave oven. The delicate flavour of the mushrooms
complements the stronger, slightly bitter flavour of the chicory. Delicious
served hot with cooked bacon or gammon steaks.*

Choux Plates filled with Seasonal Vegetables and garnished with Savoury Icing

to serve 6-8
2 cooked plates of choux pastry (recipe page 106)
700gms (1½lb) approx. mixture of cooked seasonal vegetables
chopped chives
4-6 tbls. mayonnaise (recipe page 26)
savoury icing (recipe page 106)

Mix the cooked vegetables and chives with the mayonnaise and sandwich
between the choux plates.   Spread the top with savoury icing, slice to
serve.

Choux Pastry

5fl.ozs cold water
50gms (2ozs) butter
75gms (3ozs) plain flour
2 size 1 eggs (large)

Set oven at gas 6/450°f/220°c/Aga roasting oven.
Put the water and butter into a pan and heat slowly until the butter has melted, increase the heat and when the liquid rises in the pan add the flour and beat until the mixture leaves the side of the pan, remove from heat and leave to cool a little before adding the eggs and beating until the mixture is smooth.   Lightly oil 2 baking trays and spread each with the prepared mixture shaping into plates approximately 25cms (10") in diameter. Bake in the pre-set oven for 20-30mins. or until it is puffed up and crisp. Remove from oven and serve immediately or place on a wire tray to cool.

Lazy Cook tips - choux pastry is mostly associated with éclairs or profiterole, but it has many other uses, savoury and sweet. It is a quick and easy pastry to make. The mixture can be made and kept in a refrigerator for several hours before it is baked. Always bake it in a hot oven and serve as soon as possible after it has baked, it should be crisp and light in texture.   Cooked choux can be frozen – as it begins to thaw pop it into a hot oven to bring back to a crispy texture.

Savoury Icing

2 tbls. icing sugar
1 lemon – juice and rind
few good pinches ground white pepper
few spots Worcestershire sauce
few spots cider or wine vinegar
1 tbls. freshly chopped parsley

Sieve the icing sugar into a mixing bowl, add the remaining ingredients and stir to a soft paste.

Lazy Cook tips – if it is too runny add a little more sieved icing sugar, if it is too stiff add a little warm water. The flavour should be sharp with the slightest touch of sweetness – adjust by adding more Worcestershire sauce or lemon juice.

Courgette Bake

1 courgette per person
nutmeg
sundried tomatoes
cheese – a mixture of parmesan and Shropshire blue

Set oven at gas 6/250°f/220°c/Aga roasting oven.
Wash and top and tail the courgettes before cutting into thick slices. Cook in a little boiling water for a minute or until they begin to soften, then, using a slotted spoon, put them into a shallow ovenproof dish with a tablespoon of the cooking liquid. Season with freshly grated nutmeg before scattering with slices of sundried tomatoes. Top with a mixture of Shropshire blue and parmesan cheeses. Bake, uncovered, for 10-15mins. in the pre-set oven, or under a hot grill. Serve with meat, fish or poultry, or as a light meal with fresh bread.

Lazy Cook tips – courgettes need only a little cooking but when serving them as a bake they need the initial short cooking in boiling water ('blanching'), to start the cooking process otherwise they will need a much longer time in the oven. I cut the tomatoes straight on to the courgettes with scissors. Flake, or grate the cheeses – grate the blue cheese first and the hard parmesan will clean the grater.

Courgettes (whole) with Savoury Fillings

1 or 2 courgettes per person
whole grain mustard
thin slices of – tongue, pancetta, salami, smoked ham, smoked pork or smoked salmon
radishes
spring onions
cocktail gherkins or cornichons
mayonnaise (recipe page 26)

Wash and top and tail the courgettes. Boil in a little water until they just begin to soften, remove from pan and rinse in cold water. Open by slitting lengthways taking care not to cut them into two pieces. Spread a little mustard in the opening then fill with slices of a chosen filling (folded and 'tucked' into the split), and garnish with radish slices, spring onion pieces and whole gherkins or cornichons To serve put a pot of mayonnaise in the centre of a large round serving dish (or a tray covered with foil), and arrange the filled courgettes round – like a Catherine wheel.

Lazy Cook tips – the fillings should protrude above the courgettes, choose different fillings for each courgette rather than mixing the flavours. Cornichons are similar to cocktail gherkins. Choose courgettes about 10cms (4") in length for this recipe. Serve them at the beginning of a garden party or a barbecue or serve them to start a meal. They are quick to prepare and a quantity of them looks colourful and eye-catching. A gem of a recipe especially if you have a glut of courgettes in the garden.

Fennel cooked with cream

2 fennel heads
150ml (¼pt) single cream
freshly ground white pepper

Slice the fennel and soften in approximately 50ml. (2 fl.ozs) boiling water with lid on pan. Strain off any excess liquid, add the cream and stir over a gentle heat until simmering. Season with a little freshly ground white pepper. Serve hot or cold.

Lazy Cook tips – fennel heads can also be served raw in salads. I also use the fennel 'fern' I grow in my garden to garnish savoury dishes, it is especially recommended to serve with fish. It is aniseed in flavour. See 'A Lazy Cook's Garden' (page 124).

French Beans

Wash and top and tail the beans before boiling in a little water until they are cooked to your liking. Strain off the cooking liquid (stock), and rinse the beans in cold water before serving. To serve hot, add a knob of butter to the pan and when melted stir in the cooked beans. Put into a hot dish and scatter with chopped fresh sage. Serve cold with cold meats or fish or as part of a medley of vegetables.

Marrow and Tomato au Gratin

to serve 6-8
1 marrow
fresh sage – chopped
1 x 400gm tin chopped tomatoes
pinch sugar
freshly ground white pepper
125gms (4ozs) cheese – grated
70gms (2ozs) breadcrumbs – fresh or dried

Set oven at gas 6/450°f/220°c/Aga roasting oven.
Wash and top and tail the marrow before cutting into half lengthways.
Remove the centre seeds and discard. Slice each half marrow into three
lengths and cut each of these into slices approximately 5mm (¼")
thickness. Cook in a little boiling water for about a minute to begin the
softening process then, using a slotted spoon, put them into a large shallow
ovenproof dish and scatter with chopped sage leaves. Cover with the
tinned tomatoes and juice, add a good pinch of sugar and season with
freshly ground pepper. Mix the grated cheese and breadcrumbs together
and spread over the top. Bake, uncovered, in the pre-set oven for 20-
30mins. or until it browns. Serve hot with a summer roast.

*Lazy Cook tips – this has become one of the most favourite summer
vegetables I serve. It can be prepared in advance and stored, covered, in
a refrigerator or cold larder in readiness for heating. Use a mixture of
cheeses, including a little Stilton for extra flavour – it is a good way of
using up all the bits. Always keep a supply of dried breadcrumbs (brown
or white) in store (recipe page 5), it makes the preparation of this and
many other recipes so much quicker.*

Savoury Marrow Rings
to make 6-8
1 marrow
vegetable farce (recipe page 110)
basil leaves
tomato slices
a few shavings of butter
freshly ground black pepper

Set the oven at gas 6/450°f/220°c/Aga roasting oven.

Wash and top and tail the marrow before cutting into rings approximately 2cms (1") in thickness. Remove the seedy centre and discard. Cook in a little boiling water for about a minute to begin the softening process then, using a slotted spoon, put them into a shallow ovenproof dish. Fill the centre cavity with the prepared vegetable farce, top with a basil leaf then a slice of tomato. Add a pinch sugar and season with freshly ground pepper. Top with a shaving of butter and bake in the pre-set oven, uncovered, for 10-15mins. or until hot throughout. Serve as a starter, one or two as a light meal with fresh bread, or as a vegetable accompaniment to meat, fish or poultry. Prepare in advance and store, covered, in a refrigerator or cold larder until required.

Lazy Cook tips – these are a wonderful 'Lazy Cook' standby. An excellent vegetarian recipe.

Vegetable farce

1 medium sized onion – skin and chop
1 25gms (4ozs) mushrooms – wipe and chop
1 teas. tomato purée
1 x 227gm tin chopped tomatoes
pinch sugar
1 tbls. fresh chopped herbs or 1 small teaspoon herbes de Provence
freshly ground white pepper
1-2tbls. fresh breadcrumbs – brown or white

Cook the prepared onion in a little boiling water, with lid on pan, until it begins to soften. With the exception of the breadcrumbs, stir in the remaining ingredients and simmer, without lid, until the liquid has reduced (approximately 5mins.) Stir in enough breadcrumbs to make into a moist paste. Use immediately or, when cold store, covered, in a refrigerator or cold larder, until required.

Lazy Cook tips – this is another very useful ingredient to have in store. It is excellent as a filling for fish. Dried breadcrumbs can be added but they will not absorb the moisture as readily as fresh.

Sweet and Sour Marrow

to serve 4
1 marrow
1 tbls. oil
1 pkt bacon lardons (chopped bacon)
1 medium sized onion – skin and chop
1 teas. tomato purée
1 tbls. mixed fresh chopped herbs (or 1 teas. mixed dried herbs)
6 pickled gherkins – slice
1 tbls. chutney
freshly ground while pepper
a little stock
125gms (4ozs) cheese – grated
70gms (2ozs) breadcrumbs – fresh or dried

Set the oven at gas 6/450°f/220°c/Aga roasting oven.
Wash and top and tail the marrow before cutting into half lengthways, remove the centre seeds from each half and discard. Cook each marrow half in a little boiling water, with lid on pan, until it begins to soften (this should take approximately 2-3mins.). Remove from pan and place in a roasting tin or large shallow ovenproof dish with 2tbls. of the cooking liquid, pour the remainder into a jug and keep. Wipe the pan with kitchen roll before adding 1 tbls. oil and when it is hot add the bacon lardons and onion and cook on a gentle heat until the onion softens. With the exception of the cheese and breadcrumbs, add the remaining ingredients and stir together adding a little of the cooking liquid to moisten the mixture. Pack into the pre-cooked marrow halves, top with the cheese and breadcrumbs mixed together and bake for 20-30mins. or until it is hot throughout and the top is crisp and brown. Serve with fresh bread for a substantial meal.

Lazy Cook tips – if the marrow halves are not par-boiled before being filled they will need a much longer overall baking time. Cut them in half if the marrow is too long to fit into the pan for par-boiling and put them together when transferring to the baking dish. I find a grapefruit knife is best to use when removing the centre seeds.

Baked Peppers filled with Rice, Prawns and Sundried Tomatoes

to make 4
4 red peppers
125gms (4ozs) cooked white rice (recipe page 53)
250gms (8ozs) cooked prawns
1 jar sundried tomatoes preserved in oil
2 teas. sundried tomato purée

Set oven at gas 6/450°f/220°c/Aga roasting oven.
Wash and dry the peppers before cutting off the tops (retaining the stalk), and remove all seeds.   Put a tablespoon of oil from the jar of sundried tomatoes into a shallow ovenproof dish and brush the skin of each pepper with this, including the tops.   Put into the pre-set oven and bake for 20-30mins. or until they begin to soften.   Towards the end of the cooking of the peppers heat a tablespoon of sundried tomato oil in a sauté or large frying pan, stir in the tomato purée and cook for a minute or two before adding 8 sundried tomatoes (cutting them up with scissors as they are added), the prawns and rice and stir all together.   Pack this into the cooked peppers, place lids on top and serve.

Lazy Cook tips – the combination of flavours is good.   Serve as a light meal or as a vegetable accompaniment to fish.   It is sometimes possible to buy baby sized peppers and these make excellent starters prepared and cooked in this way.

Pepper halves with a Savoury Filling

to make 8 halves
4 peppers
1-2tbls. oil
savoury filling (recipe page 118)
4 tomatoes
sugar
freshly ground white pepper
shavings of butter
fresh parsley - chopped

Set oven at gas 6/450°f/220°c/Aga roasting oven.

Wash and dry the peppers before cutting in half lengthways cutting through the green stalk, remove and discard the seeds.   Pour a tablespoon of oil into a shallow ovenproof dish, add the prepared pepper halves and brush the skins with oil, arrange skin side up and bake in the pre-set oven until they begin to soften and the skins begin to brown.   Remove from oven, turn the pepper halves over and fill each with the savoury filling.   Top with a tomato slice, a pinch of sugar and season with freshly ground white pepper, add a scattering of freshly chopped parsley and a shaving of butter and bake until hot.

Lazy Cook tips – make them from peppers of different colours. They can be cooked, and reheated on a barbecue.   Excellent as a vegetable course with meat, poultry or fish, or as a light meal or starter.   Omitting the ham from the savoury filling they can be served to vegetarians.

New Potato and Mint Pie

to serve 6
200gms pkt filo pastry
1kg (2 lbs) new potatoes
lots of fresh mint – whole leaves or chopped
freshly grated nutmeg
garlic (optional)
50gms (2ozs) approx. butter – melted

Put the potatoes into a saucepan of cold water, bring to boil and boil for 4-5mins. to commence the softening process.   Strain off the water and allow the potatoes to cool before slicing thinly.   Set oven at as 6/450°f/220°c/Aga roasting oven.   Butter well a round tin approx. 18cms (7") in diameter preferably with a loose base and line it with several layers of filo pastry leaving plenty overhanging the top.   Fill with layers of potato slices, seasoned with nutmeg, and mint, ending with potato.   Pour most of the melted butter over the top before covering with the overhanging filo pastry, brush with the remaining melted butter and bake for 20-30mins. Serve hot with fish or meat, or cold with pickle or mayonnaise and salad.

Lazy Cook tips – *you will read from the instructions on the packet that filo pastry should be kept covered with a damp cloth until it is baked to prevent it becoming brittle and difficult to handle* – *I cover it with damp kitchen roll. Have all the filling ingredients prepared before assembling the pie. If the overlapping pastry does not completely cover the top, add more layers creased into folds to make an attractive topping. When the top has browned, put a skewer into the pie to test whether the potatoes are soft, if not, reduce the oven temperature to gas 4/400°f/200°c/Aga baking oven and bake until the potatoes have softened. Buy fresh filo and any remaining can be frozen for future use.*

Spinach Crêpe

to make 4
4 crêpe (recipe below)
250gms. (8ozs) cooked spinach (recipe 115)
4 desst. single cream
freshly ground nutmeg

Put a tablespoon of cooked spinach to one side of each crêpe, top with a dessertspoon of cream and a little freshly ground nutmeg before covering with the other half to form a crescent shape. Place on a lightly oiled baking tray (or swiss roll tin), or ovenproof plate, and heat in a hot oven (gas 6/450°f/220°c/Aga roasting oven) or under a hot grill for 5-6mins. Serve as a starter.

Lazy Cook tips – *these make a good and delicate starter, or two or more can be served as a light lunch. Arranged on an ovenproof plate they can be served direct from the oven. This is just one of many ways I serve crêpe.*

Crêpe

to make approximately 24
300ml (½pt) full cream milk
100gms (4ozs) plain flour
2 large eggs
2 tbls. sunflower oil
2 tbls. cold water
butter for cooking

Put the milk into a food processor or liquidiser, add the flour, eggs and oil and process for a few seconds until smooth. Pour into a jug, cover and put in a fridge or cold larder for 30mins. to 1 hour. Take from the fridge and whisk in 2 tbls. cold water. Heat a 15cm (6") pan, smear the base with butter and pour in just enough batter to lightly coat the base (approx. 2 tbls.) When set turn it over using a wooden spatula and cook for a few seconds more before turning on to a wire tray.

Lazy Cook tips – a crêpe pan should have a heavy base which must be hot before the batter is added otherwise you will end up with a soggy mess. Spike a lump of fridge-hard butter on to a knife and use this to wipe over the base of the pan between cooking each crepe, it will give just the right amount of butter without burning fingers. Store or freeze the cold crêpe in stacks of 10 or 12 interleaving each with a piece of greaseproof. Wrap in clingfilm and use within 5 days or put into freezer bags and freeze. Defrost, or use directly from the freezer easing between the layers with a palette knife. Crêpe are another useful ingredient to have in store, especially for 'Lazy Cooks' – they can be served with savoury or sweet fillings.

Spinach – to cook

Wash the spinach leaves. Add just enough water to cover the base of a pan, add the spinach, place lid on pan, and cook over a gentle heat until the spinach has softened and reduced considerably in volume. Strain off the cooking liquid, add a nut of butter and stir over a gentle heat to dry off any excess liquid before serving. To puree, put into a food processor, or liquidiser, and process for a few seconds.

Lazy Cook tips – spinach can be cooked and stored, covered, in a refrigerator or cold larder until it is needed.

Spinach and Bacon Soufflé

I believe hot soufflés are amongst the most neglected of savoury dishes – there is a myth about them which implies they can only be produced by top chefs in expensive restaurants, this is not so, they are really very simple to prepare and bake. Read through my Lazy Cook tips and you will find how easy they are to prepare and cook and your guests will love them.

to serve 4
25gms (1 oz) butter
12gms (½oz) plain flour
500gms (1 lb) spinach (puréed)
2fl.ozs full cream milk
freshly ground white pepper
4 eggs
50gms. (2ozs) Gruyère cheese – grated
2 thick rashers cooked bacon – cut into small pieces

Set oven at gas 4/400°f/200°c/Aga baking oven.
Butter well the base and sides of an 850ml (1½pt) porcelain soufflé dish and tie a piece of buttered greaseproof or foil round the outside to project about 5cms (1") above the rim, secure the ends with a paperclip.   Stand the prepared dish on a baking tray.   Melt the butter in a large pan and remove from heat before stirring in the flour and mixing to a smooth paste (this is called a roux).   Add the milk and stir over a gentle heat until it thickens, remove from heat, season with freshly ground white pepper and stir in the spinach, cheese and bacon and finally the egg yolks.   Whisk 4 egg whites until they peak and fold them into the pan ingredients.   Pour into the prepared dish and bake for 15-20mins. or until the soufflé has risen and is firm to the touch.   Serve straight from the oven.

I first enjoyed this soufflé while staying with my husband's Auntie Margaret and family.   They lived in a beautiful château in Belgium and her cook, Blanche, travelled on her bicycle from a nearby village every afternoon to prepare and cook dinner and this soufflé was just one of the many culinary delights she cooked for us.   I felt privileged to watch her make it and although I have adjusted the method, I always enjoy making it and serving it to family and friends, it is one of the best ways of serving fresh young spinach.

Lazy Cook tips – *the secret of success is to have all the ingredients ready, the dish prepared and the oven up to temperature before beginning to make the soufflé.   As with all roux-based recipes, I recommend the butter is melted, but not hot and bubbling before the flour is added, this will ensure a smooth paste (roux) which, when all the liquid ingredients are added, can be brought to a boil and thickened.   Soufflés rise from below and if you cook by Aga place it on the floor of the baking oven.   Bring guests to the table a few minutes before the soufflé is baked while it is still well risen – test on the family so that you know roughly how long it will take to bake!*

Swiss Chard with Lemon Balm

Swiss chard
fresh lemon balm leaves
juice and rind of a lemon

Wash the chard and cut the stalks from the leaves.   Cut the stalks into chunks before adding to a little boiling water to cook, with lid on pan, for a few minutes then remove with a slotted spoon and spread over the base of a shallow ovenproof dish, scatter with lemon balm leaves and a good squeeze of lemon juice – keep warm.   Empty most of the cooking liquid from the pan (leave a smear on the base), add the leaves and cook over a gently heat, with lid on pan, until they have softened and reduced (like spinach).   Remove from heat and cut up with scissors before returning to a gentle heat and stirring until any excess liquid has evaporated.   Stir in several good squeezes of lemon juice before spreading over the stalks, scatter with grated lemon zest and serve.

Lazy Cook tips – *this can be made in advance and stored, covered, in a refrigerator or cold larder until required.   Cover to reheat in a hot oven (gas 6/450°f/220°c/Aga roasting oven) or a microwave.*

Baked Tomato Halves

Cut tomatoes in half crossways.   Sprinkle each half with a few grains of sugar before seasoning with freshly ground black pepper, a shaving of butter and a few pinches of mixed chopped fresh herbs, or dried herbes de Provence.   Put on a baking tray (or swiss roll tin) and bake in a pre-set oven (gas 6/450°f/220°c/Aga roasting oven), for 5-10mins.or until cooked, or under a hot grill.

Beef Tomatoes with a Savoury Filling

to make 4
4 beef tomatoes
4 slices bread (brown or white)
4 slices ham
4 anchovy fillets
a collection of herbs
a little oil
freshly ground pepper

Set oven at gas 6/450°f/220°c/Aga roasting oven.
Slice the top (stalk end) from the tomatoes and keep.   Remove the pips
and centre core, put these into a sieve to drain off the juices.   Put the
bread, ham, anchovy and herbs into a food processor with some freshly
ground pepper and the drained tomato juices and process to a sticky paste.
Pack this filling into the tomato cavities and cover with the reserved tops.
Lightly oil a shallow ovenproof dish, add the tomatoes and lightly oil these
all over before baking in the pre-set oven for 15-20mins. or until baked.
Serve hot, warm or cold as a starter or a light meal.

*Lazy Cook tips – I remove the centre core and pips using a grapefruit
knife.   These tomatoes can also be prepared and cooked on a barbecue.
Serve with salad and fresh bread for a delicious lunch, use slightly smaller
tomatoes if serving as a starter.*

Cherry Tomatoes with a Savoury Filling

to fill 20 tomatoes
20 cherry tomatoes
2 slices bread (brown or white) – break into pieces
3 fresh apricots – remove stones, slice flesh
4 anchovies
10 or more fresh basil leaves
1 teas. fresh lemon juice
freshly ground pepper
sweet basil dressing – optional (recipe page 119)

Cut the rounded end from each tomato and keep. Using a small teaspoon scoop out the centre flesh and put, with any juices into a sieve. Put the remaining ingredients into a food processor, or liquidiser, with any juices from the tomatoes and process together then spoon into the tomatoes and top with the cut off ends. Serve as starters with a little salad and a sweet basil dressing, or arrange them on a large plate and serve as canapés.

Lazy Cook tips – by cutting off the rounded end of these small tomatoes, the stalk end will enable them to sit firmly on a plate. Should the paste be crumbly, add a little more lemon juice. To add to the presentation a small basil leaf can be tucked into the paste before the top is replaced, and a few nasturtium flowers can be dotted around the plate. Use anchovies preserved in oil and available by weight from most supermarkets or delicatessen. A refreshing and attractive way to serve these little tomatoes.

Sweet Basil Dressing

3 tbls. cider or wine vinegar
8 tbls. oil
freshly ground white pepper
lots of fresh basil leaves – break into pieces

Shake all the ingredients together in a lidded jar. Store and use within 4 days.

Ovcn dried Tomatoes

tomatoes
oil
sugar
sprigs of fresh rosemary

Cut fresh tomatoes in half (removing pips is optional). Place on an oiled baking tray, and brush each tomato with oil. Add a pinch of sugar then cover with fresh rosemary. Put in a very low oven until dry (approximately 24hrs.). When cold put into jars and fill with oil – discard the rosemary.

Turnips with Lemon

young turnips
1 lemon

Top and tail the turnips and scrub the skins.   Slice thinly and cook in a
little boiling water until they begin to soften.   Strain off the cooking liquid
and keep for stock, add lemon juice to the pan and stir the turnip slices in
this over a gentle heat.   Pile into a dish and scatter with grated lemon zest
to serve.

Vegetable Flan with a Savoury Jelly topping served with Orange Mayonnaise

to serve 6-8
1 ready cooked pastry case
300ml (½pt) bechamel sauce (recipe page 121)
selection of crisply cooked vegetables – cold
300ml (½pt) savoury jelly (recipe page 23)
orange mayonnaise (recipe page 26)

Make the jelly in a jug and when cold allow it to 'begin' to set.   Spread the
sauce over the base of the pastry case and arrange the chosen vegetables on
top.   Cover with the jelly and smooth the top with a palette knife dipped in
hot water. Serve in slices when the jelly has completely set.

Lazy Cook tips *– for good presentation choose a selection of colourful
vegetables which can be cooked whole or sliced, and arrange them so that
when it is served each slice will be similar.   This is a most attractive flan
to serve and will be very popular with your guests, especially vegetarians
when the jelly should be made with Gelezone (vegetarian gelatine) – follow
the manufacturer's instructions for making.*

Béchamel Sauce

300ml. (½pt) milk
a piece of mace
bayleaf
slice of onion
4 peppercorns
25gms (1 oz) butter
25gms (1 oz) plain flour
1 tbls. single cream

Put the milk, mace, bay leaf, onion and peppercorns into a pan and bring to a simmer over a low heat.   Remove from heat, cover the pan and leave for 5-6 minutes.   Melt the butter in a pan, add the flour and mix to a paste (this is known as a 'roux').   Strain the seasoned milk on to the roux and stir continuously over a gentle heat until the sauce simmers and thickens then stir in the cream.   Serve hot or cold.

Lazy Cook tips – I do not often make 'roux' based sauce recipes nowadays but béchamel is a delicious sauce on it's own or as a foundation for many other sauces when other ingredients can be added, i.e. grated cheeses or herbs   I recommend the butter is melted, but not hot and bubbling, before the flour is added.   This will ensure a smooth paste (roux) which, when all the liquid ingredients are added, can be brought to a boil and thickened. If lumps should occur, remove the pan from the heat and whisk until they dissolve.   These ingredients will make a thick sauce which, when cold will be of the right consistency for the Vegetable Flan (recipe page 120), to thin it down, add more cream, milk or stock.

Orange Mayonnaise

mayonnaise (recipe page 26)
1 fresh orange – juice and rind

Follow the mayonnaise recipe but before adding the oil add the juice of one orange and stir in the grated zest when the mayonnaise has reached the desired consistency.

Vegetable Terrine

to serve 8-10 slices
2 red peppers
2 yellow peppers
225gms (8 ozs) spinach – wash and dry
4 large flat mushrooms – wipe with damp kitchen paper
8 artichokes (bought by weight from a delicatessen counter)
freshly grated nutmeg
1 tbls fresh parsley - chopped
1 teas. fresh thyme - chopped
freshly ground white pepper
1 tbls. lemon juice

Set oven at gas 6/450°f/220°c/Aga roasting oven.   Lightly oil a 900gm. (2 lb) loaf tin.   Wash and dry the peppers before cutting off the tops (discard the stalk only), and cutting each pepper into quarters, remove seeds and cut off any white fleshy bits and discard.   Line the base of the tin with the red peppers, skin side down, cutting partway down each quarter to encourage it to flatten during cooking.   Cover with half the spinach and season with freshly grated nutmeg, parsley and thyme. Remove the stalks from the mushrooms and lay the mushrooms, skin side uppermost, on top of the spinach using the stalks and cut pieces of mushroom to fill in any gaps, season with freshly ground white pepper. Cover with artichoke hearts and cover these with the remaining spinach. Season with grated nutmeg, parsley and thyme and pour on the lemon juice.   Finally cover with the yellow peppers, skin side uppermost, cutting partway down each quarter to encourage it to flatten during cooking. Press the ingredients down with your hand then cover with buttered greaseproof and seal with foil.   Stand the tin on a baking tray and bake in the pre-set oven for ¾ - 1hr. or until the ingredients have reduced or, when pierced with a metal skewer they feel cooked.   Remove from oven and pour off any excess liquid.   Leave in the tin for 5mins. before loosening the sides with a palette knife and turning on to a serving dish.   Slice to serve, hot or cold.

Lazy Cook tips – this terrine is quickly assembled and can be stored, covered, in a refrigerator or cold larder until you wish to bake it. Although the tin may appear over full, the ingredients shrink considerably during baking – tie a string around the tin to hold the foil in place if you feel it is necessary. This is colourful and delicious terrine to serve as a main course or a starter, or as a vegetable accompaniment to meat, poultry or fish. Artichokes can be bought by weight at delicatessen counters, or in jars. If using dried herbs, use half the quantity stated.

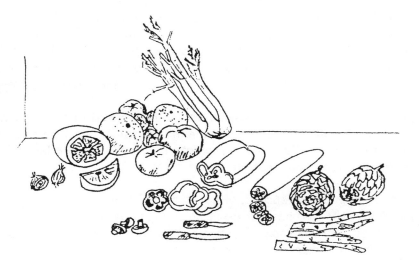

A LAZY COOK'S GARDEN

In summer my enthusiasm for fresh summer flavours takes me out of the kitchen and into the garden. Despite the variety and the quality of summer ingredients now available, for me, nothing compares with the flavour of produce picked from the garden and put straight into the pot. But, 'small is beautiful' is my advice! Grow just a few of your favourite summer ingredients and buy the remainder from your usual supplier.

I was a late-comer to gardening and I am still very much an amateur but I enjoy it so much that I cannot imagine ever not wanting to garden. Gardening, like cooking, is never a chore to me, weeding gives me as much pleasure as digging the first early potatoes. Truth to tell, it is my love of gardening that has contributed to my becoming so 'lazy' a cook! Often I will go into the garden for "a little potter" only to hear the church clock chime five and remember we have friends coming to supper and nothing is prepared!

I think of the garden as an extension to the house and I have divided ours into a number of sitting areas, like rooms in the house. With ever increasing demands on my time, I have also attempted to make it more labour saving and I am forever designing 'another' paved area!

In addition to plants and shrubs, of greater importance to me are the small greenhouse and the two small beds in which I grow herbs, salads and just a few vegetables. These I know will not only add refreshing flavour, colour and texture to my summer recipes, but such ingredients will enable me to transform a very simple meal into something special at the snip of the scissors or the washing of a few leaves.

Early potatoes and runner beans occupy one of the beds, and in the second I grow several varieties of 'cut and come again' lettuce – they grow so tall that by the end of the season I have to stake them! Other salad ingredients, herbs, and a few vegetables also share this bed. Dotted amongst the flower beds and shrubs rest the perennial herbs - sage, fennel, chives, lemon balm, rosemary and marjoram. In addition, nasturtiums (for their leaves and flowers), and, wild strawberries – those precious little jewels which enhance the flavour and presentation of my recipes sweet and savoury.

All of these play an important part in my summer cooking but before listing them and a few hints on growing and using them in cooking, here's an important tip – help everything you plant grow bigger and better by keeping a compost heap. All uncooked vegetation can be composted down to make your very own feed.

HERBS

Herbs will add colour and fragrance to a garden.   Many varieties make excellent ground cover and will deter some pests.   Choose seed packets which state 'for modern gardeners', or 'for go-ahead gardeners'.   To save space sow the seeds in small pots (roughly 8-10cms (3"-4") and as they grow they can be pricked out into larger trays for growing on into seedlings and transplanting into pots or into the soil.   Read and follow the growers instructions and advice on the reverse of the packet.   A few herb leaves are best served whole or torn, but the flavour of most herbs develops as they are chopped.

ANNUALS

SWEET BASIL – *large fragrant leaves, spicy in flavour with a hint of clove.*

I transplant several seedlings into medium sized pots and place them around the garden and on my kitchen windowsill – they like as much sun as they can get.   Use as a flavouring in cooking, or as a garnish with tomatoes, eggs, rice, pasta, and salads.   Use whole leaves or break into pieces.

LEAF CORIANDER - *flat fragrant leaves (not dis-similar to flat leafed parsley) but with a sharp earthy flavour.   The fragrance will remain on your fingers long after picking.*

I plant the seeds into well raked soil.   Grows best in a sunny, dry spot. Use in soups and sauces, in salads, and with fish and poultry.

LAND CRESS - *flat leaves which grow on short stems in clusters.   Hot and peppery in flavour, not dis-similar to watercress.*

Since discovering this a few years ago it has become a great favourite.   I sow the seeds directly into the soil.   Kept moist it will grow in profusion well into the autumn.   Pick regularly and serve the leaves on the tender stem.   It will give character to a mixed green salad or serve it as a garnish drizzled with a little walnut oil dressing.   I have also added it, cut up, into soups and sauces.   Add, sparingly, to courgette and marrow recipes.

PARSLEY – *curly and flat leafed, the strongest flavour is in the stem which is often discarded.*
I have to say I am not very successful at growing parsley either in pots or directly into the soil and I depend on kind neighbours to supply me with it in 'quantity'.   Whole leaves are excellent as a garnish, or chopped they will enhance the flavour of almost any dish, salad or sauce - 'parsley sauce' being one of the best known, I like this made with so much parsley that it turns green in colour.

ROCKET - *leaves have a hot, dry taste, quite unlike any other herb.*
I sow this directly into the soil and also in pots.   Pick the young leaves regularly for continual growth and use as a garnish, with green salads, and with egg dishes.

PERENNIALS

BAY LEAVES - *dark green shiny leaves when growing which become pale in colour when dried.   Strong in flavour.*
I mostly use whole dried bay leaves in steak and kidney pie, with mince and other beef and game recipes and marinades.   I also add them to vegetable soups.   Use sparingly, they will dominate the flavour of delicate foods.

CHIVES - *reed-like green stems with a mild onion flavour.*
I use these with egg recipes, in salads, and as a garnish.   Add at the last minute to cooked dishes to preserve the flavour and colour.   Snip with scissors into the required lengths.

FENNEL - *(fern) - a strong anise flavour, not dis-similar to dill in flavour and appearance.*
I grow this for the leaves which in my recipes I refer to as 'fennel fern'. Use as a delicate garnish with fish or add a little to a salad – use sparingly, it has a dominant flavour.   If the plant is allowed to grow tall, it will grow large yellow flowers in late summer, these add interest and fragrance to a flower arrangement.

LEMON BALM - *green and yellow varieties can be grown, each has a delicate lemon aroma and flavour.*
Used mostly in salads and drinks.

MARJORAM and OREGANO - *two herbs of different appearance but with a similar spicy flavour.*

Marjoram is slightly more delicate in flavour than Oregano I mostly use these in mixed chopped herbs. The delicate leaves, lime green in colour, are excellent in small flower arrangements.

MINTS – *many varieties are available, but 'spearmint' is the one most commonly used in cooking.*

Take care, mints will quickly take over the garden. They are often grown in a container sunk into a bed, or in individual large pots when they will need regular watering in a dry season. A most useful herb with a variety of flavours. Add a sprig to fruit cups, and use as a garnish with many savoury and sweet dishes. Chopped mint complements the flavours of new potatoes and garden peas. I serve mint sauce with roast lamb; both mints sauce and mint jelly give an instant piquant flavour when added to savoury sauces.

NASTURTIUM – *brightly coloured flowers which grow well in poor soil.*

Grow in pots or tubs or directly into the soil where they will cascade and spread. I use the flowers to decorate summer puddings and gateaux, but both leaves and flowers can be added to salads. A great plant to grow.

ROSEMARY - *small sharp leaves with a pinewood aroma*

This grows as a bush-like plant which produces small white flowers towards the end of summer. I use this mostly with lamb and tuck a few twigs beneath a joint to be roasted. I also add it to tomato-based recipes, soups and sauces. The needle-type leaves can be used whole or cut up – a lovely herb.

SAGE - *has a strong distinctive flavour*

Another favourite of mine and one which I feel is under-rated. Sage and Onion stuffing is a popular accompaniment to roast pork. I also add it to seasoned flour for coating individual pork steaks or chops before sealing. I add it to sauces to serve with pork. I also serve it with broad beans, and marrow recipes. Purple sage is a good ground cover and produces small pink flowers.

TARRAGON - *leaves have a fairly strong spicy, anise flavour.*
Make sure to grow 'French' tarragon for aroma and flavour. Other varieties will grow in profusion but they have no flavour. This is another much loved herb which I have difficulty growing and reserve the few leaves I am able to pick for garnish. I have, as yet, not succeeded in keeping it through the winter and I buy a new plant each spring. An excellent herb when dried and this is how I use it in many of my recipes.

THYME - *a small plant with tiny leaves*
.Of the many varieties lemon thyme is possibly the one most commonly used in cooking. Use thyme in almost any dishes, and with other herbs. Thyme and parsley stuffing is a favourite of mine and I serve it with poultry. A small herb but a much loved one.

WILD STRAWBERRIES – *small in leaf and fruit and a real gem in summer.*
I attempt to restrict these to one small bed, and overhanging walls but they will pop up all over the garden and need controlling. My summer recipes wouldn't be nearly as exciting without them, I use them all the time in savoury and sweet dishes.

SALADS

LAMB'S LETTUCE/CORN SALAD – *dark green leaves slightly hot in flavour.*
I grow this directly into the soil. Pick the leaves when young, they become bitter and tough as they grow stronger. Use whole leaves in a mixed green salad, or use as a garnish.

LETTUCE - I grow lettuces of different shapes and colours, but they all have to be the 'cut and come again' varieties which avoids continuous planting and will provide lettuce throughout the summer. Buy seeds which say 'for go-ahead gardeners' on the packet.

TOMATOES - I grow cherry tomatoes of which there are many varieties. Grown in pots on a sunny terrace, they look as attractive and colourful as the flowers, and they have an added advantage – they can be eaten! Grow red and yellow ones and serve the very tiny ones whole with drinks before a meal. The aroma from a freshly picked tomato is a culinary delight to be experienced!

VEGETABLES

BEANS – FRENCH AND RUNNERS - I grow climbing, and dwarf ('purple Queen') varieties of French beans. For later picking I grow what I call 'English' beans commonly known as runner's, stick or kidney beans. The are all good.

COURGETTES - Because these plants need a sunny position and a lot of space I am usually limited to two plants only.   Water and feed them well and pick regularly for a continuous supply of courgettes.   I allow one or two to grow on and cook them as I do marrow, they have a denser flesh and a more tender and tasty skin.

POTATOES - Seed potatoes need to be purchased in January and kept in an airy, light, frost free room to develop the shoots (this is called 'chitting') – I stand the potatoes on egg trays to keep them set apart and to protect the young shoots   Take advice and buy the varieties which suit the soil in your area.   Potatoes dug from the garden and put straight into the pot have a superb flavour.

SPINACH - Perpetual Leaf Beat and cut and come again are both popular. Pick the tender young leaves and add to salads.   An excellent vegetable that can be picked well into the Autumn

SWISS CHARD - I grow a little of this because it is not always possible to buy it.   I cook the stalk and leaves separately and serve them with the leaves at the top.   It is a tasty vegetable, the leaves are similar in appearance and flavour to spinach, but there is the added flavour of the stalk.

COOKERY ABREVIATIONS AND TERMS
(A Lazy Cook's Shorthand)

au gratin - a topping of cheese and breadcrumbs, usually over a sauce or cooked vegetables.

Blanche – to cook in boiling water for a short time, to whiten.

Bain-marie – a water bath in which certain foods are baked inside or on top of the oven to prevent them drying or cooking too quickly. Also useful for keeping certain sauces hot before serving.

b/b – bread and butter

b/c's – breadcrumbs

Boil – lots of bubbles

Par boil – to put ingredients into cold water and bring to a boil

Rapid boil – lots of bubbles rising in the pan

Bouchée – small cases made from puff pastry served with savoury or sweet fillings, cold or hot

Celery – a head = the whole celery
a stick = a piece from the celery head

Chine – to remove the bone from a joint of meat, usually best end or loin of lamb, so that individual chops can be cut.

Degorger – to extract strong flavours

Desst. – dessertspoon

f.g.p. – freshly ground pepper

Fillet – to remove all bones

To extract flavour – cut ingredients small and cook slowly as in soup, chutney and jam making.

To seal in flavour – to brown ingredients quickly in hot fat

g/a's – ground almonds

Gratinée – a topping of breadcrumbs

Green – unsmoked, usually refers to ham or bacon

Knead – when handling bread dough

Knead Lightly – when handling pastry or scone dough

Marinade – to leave in soak, often in a brine of wine, oil and herbs

p.f. – plain flour

Pate – a pastry or dough

Paté – a savoury paste

Press – to stand a weight on cooked or prepared food

Purée – ingredients made smooth by liquidising, processing or passing through a sieve

Roulade – to roll

Roux – a paste made from butter and flour as a base for a sauce

s & p – salt and pepper

Sauté – to cook quickly in hot fat

Seasoned flour - plain flour with either salt, pepper, herbs or other ingredients added. Used for coating ingredients before they are cooked to prevent sticking or to introduce additional flavours

s/d toms – sun-dried tomatoes

s.r. – self-raising flour

Simmer – gentle bubbles

Simmer gently – occasional bubbles

Sweat – to soften vegetables in butter with lid on pan

tbls. - tablespoon

teas. – teaspoon

t.o.m. – top of milk

HOB TEMPERATURES

Gentle simmer – an occasional bubble
Simmer – a more regular bubble
Boil – constant bubbles
Rapid boil – constant bubbles rising in pan

Aga owners should start the simmering process on the hobs then transfer the pan to the simmering oven.

OVEN TEMPERATURES

These can vary considerably and the temperatures given below, and the ones quoted in the recipes in this book, should be used as guidelines and adjusted according to your cooker.

	Gas	F	C	Aga
Warm	1–2	25°-250°	10°-120°	bottom left (4-oven)
Moderate/ Simmering	3-4	250°-350°	120°-160°	top left (4-oven)
Baking	4-5	375°-400°	180°-200°	top (2-oven) bottom R (4-oven)
Roasting	6-7	450°-500°	220°-250°	top (2-oven) top R (4-oven)

2-oven Aga owners can reduce the oven temperature by using the large baking sheet, a cake-baker, or bain-marie (please refer to booklet supplied by Aga).

WEIGHTS and MEASURES

as used in recipes in this book

Dry measurements

25gms	=	1 oz
50gms	=	2 ozs
100gms	=	4 ozs
175gms	=	6 ozs
225gms	=	8 ozs
700gms	=	1½ lbs
900gms	=	2 lbs
1 kg	=	2 lbs 4 ozs
1¾ kg	=	4 lbs

Liquid measurements

100ml	=	4 fl.ozs
150ml	=	¼ pint (1 gill)
300ml	=	½ pint
425ml	=	¾ pint
600ml	=	1 pint
1 litre	=	1¾ pints
1¾ ltrs	=	3 pints

RECOMMENDED UTENSILS

Remember a good chopping board and a sharp knife are the basic tools of the trade. In addition only buy equipment that will take the drudgery out of the preparation of ingredients always putting 'quality' before 'quantity'. A food processor is essential for 'lazy cooking' and a free-standing liquidiser/blender is also an asset. A selection of pots and pans and casseroles of the best quality you can afford. Other standard equipment should include baking trays, wire cooling trays, a grater, various spoons and ladles. A measuring jug, wooden spoons and spatulas.

Purchase a variety of colourful serving dishes and plates and, if you are fortunate enough to have inherited them, take Granny's lovely old plates and dishes out of the cupboard and use them to show off your meals.

RECOMMENDED STORE CUPBOARD

The choice of store cupboard is a personal one but in addition to basic cupboard, fridge and freezer ingredients, I recommend the following many of which will be needed for the recipes in this book.

BAKING INGREDIENTS
Baking powder
Breadcrumbs – dried (brown or white)
Flour – a selection - (I always use plain flour and add baking powder
   adding 1 teas. per 25gm. (1 oz) flour.
Pastry – ready made cases, filo, puff, shortcrust

SUGARS/SWEETENERS – a selection

BISCUITS/CONFECTIONERY
Selection including Amaretti and Trifle sponges

DAIRY PRODUCTS
To include bacon, butter, cheeses, eggs

DRIED FRUITS – a selection to include apricots and prunes

DRINKS
Coffee – fresh beans and instant
Fruit juices and syrups - bottles and small tins

ESSENCES/FLAVOURINGS
Almond, Vanilla, Vanilla sticks

HERBS (Dried)
To include – bay leaves, herbes de Provence, mint, sage, tarragon

MUSTARDS and SEASONINGS
Selection of mustards
Bottled sauces, including mushroom ketchup

NUTS - a selection

JAMS/PRESERVES
Selection of jams, lemon curd, jelly's, marmalade

PICKLES/PRESERVES
anchovies preserved in oil (bought by weight) – store in fridge
capers, cocktail gherkins, cocktail onions
olives – pitted, black or green – store in fridge
sundried tomatoes preserved in oil
tomato purée

PASTA/RICE - selection of shapes and flavours

SPICES - selection of ground and whole

LIQUEURS/WINES
Wines – red, white, sparkling
Liqueurs to include – Amaretto, Benedictine, Brandy, Crème de Cacao,
Grand Marnier,
Pimm's
Sherry – sweet, medium, dry

OILS/VINEGARS
Oils - selection to include walnut
Vinegars – selection to include balsamic, cider, tarragon, wine

TINS
A selection of savoury and sweet
Soups – to include Bisque (crab and lobster), Condensed
Tomatoes – all sizes

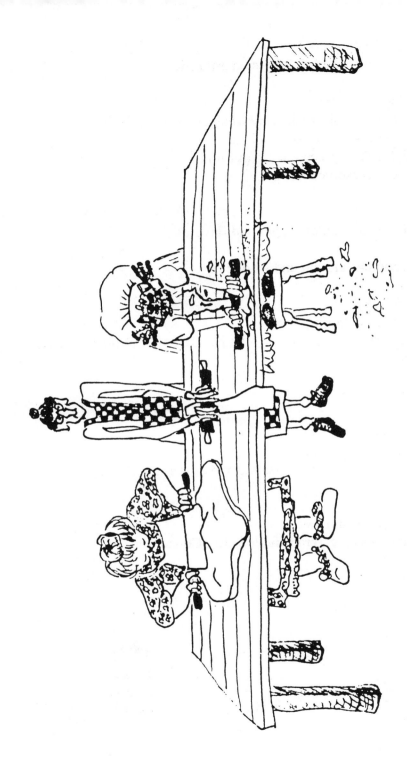

Pastry Rolling Competition

COMPLETE INDEX

BISCUITS/BREADS/CAKES/PASTRY

Biscuits –   Page

Almond	1
Chocolate and Cinnamon	1
Lemon	2
Spicy Fruit	2

Breads and Rolls –

Breadcrumbs	5
Evy's Fruit Loaf	3
White Rolls and Bread	4
Wholemeal Rolls and Bread	5

Cakes –

Chocolate/Gateau	6
Coffee and Cinnamon	6
Lemon	7
Lemon Sandwich/Gateau	8
Roulade	25
Shortbread Plates	75
Sponge Drops, Fingers and Plates	65

Pastry –

Bases	9
Choux	106

CANAPÉS

Cherry Tomatoes with a Savoury Filling	118
Chicken Liver Parcels	90
Fresh Salmon Bake	26
Melon and Fruit Sticks	9
Pastry Bases topped with Herb Cheese and Fresh Strawberries	10
Pastry Bases topped with Savoury Butter, Black Pudding & Tomato	10
Pastry Bases topped with Savoury Butter, Ox Tongue & Cornichons	10

COOKERY ABBREVIATIONS AND TERMS   130-131

DRINKS/CUPS

Drinks –

Elderflower Cordial	12
Herb flavoured water	12
Iced Coffee	13
Lemonade	13

Wine Cups –

Pimm's 14
Sparkling Cup 14
Summer Sunshine 14

FISH
Cod Fillet baked with Almonds and served with a Fresh Plum Sauce 15
Concertinas of Fish 16
Fish Pudding 16
Gurnard baked with a Savoury filling 17
Herring Fillets baked in Orange Juice 18
Mackerel Fillets baked in White Wine 19
Mediterranean Fish Pie 20
Prawn and Melon Platter 21
Salmon Baked Whole 22
Salmon served with a Savoury Jelly garnish 22
Salmon Bake 26
Salmon Millefeuille 24
Salmon Roulade 24
Smoked Salmon and Prawn Parcels with a Creamed Pepper Sauce 27
Trout Fillets with Fresh Strawberries and Fresh Thyme 27
Tuna Steaks with a Spicy Cream Sauce 28

HOB TEMPERATURES 132
ICINGS/JELLIES/SYRUPS
Lemon Icing 8
Savoury Icing 106
Water Icing 74
Savoury Jelly 23
Sugar Syrup 70

LAZY COOK'S GARDEN 124-129
MEAT AND POULTRY
Chicken Breasts with Bacon Strips and Cherry Tomatoes 31
Chicken Jubilee 32
Chicken Liver Parcels 90
Chicken Millefeuille 33
Chicken Thighs with Fresh Coriander and Bacon 34
Ham and Bacon joints - to cook 35
Ham or Bacon with Broad Beans and Coriander 36
Ham with a Mediterranean Sauce 36
Bacon and Parsley Sauce 37
Ham Platter for a Buffet Table 38
Lamb Cutlets with a Quick Tomato Sauce 39

Lamb Fillets with Redcurrants and Garden Mint 40
Lamb with Orange and Rosemary and a Brandy Sauce 41
Lambs Liver – Summer 42
Pork Fillet with a Burnt Pepper Sauce 43
Pork Steaks with Peach Halves 44
Pork Terrine 45
Turkey and Mushroom Terrine 46

OVEN TEMPERATURES 132

PASTA/RICE
Pasta with Chicken and Fresh Apricots and Lemon Balm 48
Pasta with Chicken Livers 49
Pasta with Summer Vegetables in a Mediterranean Cream Sauce 51
Rice - To Cook 53
Rice - Summer Savoury 52
Sweetcorn Rice 102

PRESERVES
Chutney –
Damson 56
Plum 56
Jam –
Apricot 58
Damson 58
Plum 59
Raspberry 59
Strawberry 60
Making – things to remember 57
Test for a set 57
Vinegar -
Blackberry or Raspberry 61

PUDDINGS
Baked Egg Custard 79
Crème Caramel 62
Fruit compote 64
Gateau – Chocolate and Strawberry 62
          Royale 64
Meringues – basic recipe 66
Mini Raspberry Meringues 67
Praline Meringue 67
Praline Powder 68
Strawberry Meringue Ring 68

Shapes - Meringue bases and plates 66
    Meringues petites 66
    Meringue rings 66
Nectarine and Brandy Pie 69
Peaches poached with Amaretto Cream 70
Plum and Almond Pudding 71
Rhubarb stewed 72
Rhubarb and Strawberry Crumble 71
Sorbet – Elderflower 73
    Lemon 73
Sponge Plates 65
Strawberry Millefeuille 74
Strawberry Shortbread with fresh Apricot Sauce 75
Shortbread Plates 75
Summer Pudding 76
Trifles – Blackcurrant 77
    Traditional made with Peaches and Brandy 78
    Upsidedown Peach 79
    Upsidedown Strawberry 80
RECOMMENDED STORE CUPBOARD 134-135
RECOMMENDED UTENSILS 133
SALADS
Beetroot 81
Green – mixed 81
Potato (1) 82
Potato (2) 82
Tomato - mixed 83
Tomato and fresh Basil 83
SAUCES / FILLINGS / PASTES
Savoury Sauces–
Bechamel 121
Burnt Pepper 44
Creamed Pepper 27
Mayonnaise – basic recipe 26
Mayonnaise - Orange 121
Mediterranean 36
Mediterranean Cream 51
Parsley 37
Quick Tomato 39
Spicy Cream 29

Sweet Basil Dressing 119
Vinaigrette 82

Sweet Sauces –
Caramel 63
Fresh Apricot 76
Fresh Plum 15

Fillings and Pastes
Parsley and Thyme Stuffing 47
Savoury Filling (1) 118
Savoury Filling (2) 118
Savoury Paste 18
Vegetable Farce 110

SOUPS AND STOCKS

Soup – Courgette and Orange 85
Courgette and Tomato 86
Melon and Ginger 86
Pea and Ham 87
Summer Vegetable 88

Stock – Fish 89
Ham 89
Meat 89
Vegetable 89

STARTERS AND LIGHT MEALS

Cherry Tomatoes with a Savoury filling 118
Chicken Liver Parcels 90
Courgettes with Savoury fillings 107
Egg Mayonnaise with Anchovies and (Wild) Strawberries 91
Eggs in Savoury Jelly 91
Fresh Herb and (Wild) Strawberry Loaf 92
Fresh Salmon bake 26
Kebabs - mini 93
Onion flan 94
Pastry bases topped with Herb Cheese and fresh Strawberries 10
Pastry bases topped with Savoury Butter, Black Pudding & Tomato 10
Pastry bases topped with Ox Tongue and Cornichons 10
Pitta Parcels with Mushrooms & Baby Sweetcorn perfumed with
Fennel Fern 95
Pitta Parcels with Summer Salad and a Herb Vinaigrette 95
Prawn and Melon Platter 21
Salmon Bake 26

Sandwiches presented on a large platter 96

Savoury Cheesecake Slices 97

Spinach with Bacon and Tomato Concertinas 98

VEGETABLES

Asparagus 100

Aubergine baked with Mushrooms and Fresh Thyme 101

Aubergine slices with Parmesan Cheese 102

Aubergine slices with Sweetcorn Rice 102

Beetroot – to cook 103

Beetroots – roasted 103

Beetroots (whole) with fresh Tarragon 104

Broad beans 104

Carrots (whole) with Pumpkin Seeds 104

Chicory – baked 105

Choux Plates filled with Vegetables with Savoury Icing Garnish 105

Courgette Bake 107

Courgettes (whole) with Savoury Fillings 107

Fennel cooked with cream 108

French Beans 108

Marrow and Tomato au Gratin 109

Marrow – savoury rings 109

Marrow – sweet and sour 111

Peppers filled with Rice, Prawns and Sundried Tomatoes 112

Pepper halves with a Savoury Filling 112

Potato and Mint pie 113

Spinach – to cook 115

Spinach and Bacon Souffle 115

Spinach Crêpe 114

Sweetcorn Rice 102

Swiss Chard with Lemon Balm 117

Tomatoes – Beef with a Savoury Filling 118

Tomatoes – Cherry with a Savoury Filling 118

Tomatoes – halves baked 117

Tomatoes – oven dried 119

Turnips with Lemon 120

Vegetable Flan with a Savoury Jelly topping, served with
Orange Mayonnaise 120

Vegetable Terrine 122

WEIGHTS AND MEASURES 133